EROTIC

LIFESTYLES

IRIS AND

STEVEN FINZ

REAL PEOPLE DISCUSS

THEIR UNUSUAL

SEXUAL PRACTICES

ST. MARTIN'S PRESS ✄ NEW YORK

www.stmartins.com

Library of Congress Cataloging-in-Publication Data

Finz, Iris.
    Erotic lifestyles : real people discuss their unusual sexual practices / Iris and Steven Finz.
        p. cm.
    ISBN 0-312-30149-9
        1. Sex—Case studies. 2. Sex customs—Case studies. I. Finz, Steven. II. Title.

HQ21.F64 2004
306.7—dc22

                                                                    2003058540

First Edition: February 2004

10 9 8 7 6 5 4 3 2 1

To all the people who shared their stories
with us and our readers so that the world
would better understand their erotic lifestyles

CONTENTS

$\mathscr{I}$NTRODUCTION

One of the things a child finds hard to accept when growing up is that not all people are the same. We tend to expect that others will see everything the same way we do, will think the same way we do, and will feel exactly the way we do about things. Learning that this is not so is part of the process of maturation. It comes from observing the world around us and recognizing the diversity that makes it so wondrous.

We do not usually have an opportunity to observe the sexual activities of others, however. So we tend to believe that what works for us works for everyone, and what does not work for us cannot possibly work for anyone. When we encounter an erotic preference that does not correspond with our own, we are like Shakespeare's character Horatio exclaiming, "This is wondrous strange." This book is intended to be like Hamlet's answer, "There are more things in heaven and earth, Horatio, than are dreamt of in your philosophy."

We write books about sex, all kinds of sex. We have published six of them about the sexual behavior of real people. We are not psychologists or sociologists or any other kind of "-ologists"—just interested, nonjudgmental listeners and observers. This has encouraged large numbers of people to tell us their most private secrets, secure in the knowledge that we will be attentive and report accurately on what we hear without forming any negative opinions or expressing any disapproval.

Sometimes, we are so certain that we already have heard everything that we find ourselves shaking our heads in surprise upon learning the intimate details of the lives of other people. Like Horatio, we are tempted to think it wondrously strange. Almost invariably, however, we find that the person telling us some unexpected erotic tale is just one of many who share his or her unusual preference. We begin to ask questions, we begin to do research, and soon we discover that there is an organization or even an entire subculture consisting of people with similar sexual interests, people who have found ways to make their uncommon patterns of behavior part of their everyday lives.

We are fascinated by the diversity of erotic lifestyles and we believe that you will be equally intrigued. The nature of our work allows us to explore them, to gather information that otherwise might be unavailable to our readers. We do not endorse any of the practices about which we write, nor do we suggest that you experiment with them. If you are motivated to do so, you probably will, with or without our prompting. If not, we believe you can gain a great deal just by knowing how your neighbors secretly behave. We hope this will widen your perspective, as it has ours.

Understanding the erotic lifestyles of others has made us more tolerant of our fellow human beings. It has even helped us realize that our own fascination with details of the sex lives of others is a somewhat unusual sexual preference. By building our work around that fascination, we too have developed what some might call a bizarre erotic lifestyle. Recognizing that, we could not possibly profess to pass judgment on others.

As always, we do not attempt to draw any statistical conclusions from our research or to say what percentage of the general population lives in any particular way. We are not so naive as to think it is ever possible to find a truly random sample from which general conclusions can be drawn about sexuality. We are not so desperately eager to revolutionize established thought in the world of social science as to pretend that we believe the people who tell their stories are always honest with themselves or with us. In our opinions, those who base theories about sexual behavior on what they hear from informants are not always to be trusted for this reason.

Our studies are anecdotal. We listen to what we hear and retell it without making any major changes in the language originally used. We do change names and facts enough to make it impossible for anyone to recognize the people involved. We feel we learn a great deal from these individual stories and hope you will feel the same way. At the very least, you will find them entertaining, as you discover that there is more in heaven and earth than was dreamt of in your philosophy.

1

LOOK AT MY BODY

MOST OF US LIKE SHOWING OFF. WINNING A SANDLOT baseball game is important, but the best thing about hitting a home run may be knowing that the people in the stands will see how skillful we are. When we buy our clothes, we stand in front of mirrors trying to imagine what others will think when they see us. Some of us pick tight or revealing garments so that everyone can see how sexy we are.

Movie actors and runway models manage to make a career out of their exhibitionism. For most people, however, the thrill of being looked at is only an occasional pleasure, associated with summer days at the beach or attendance at functions requiring formal attire. Those rare opportunities are usually enough.

There are some, however, who feel a need to display themselves every day. It gives their lives a special meaning, making them confident of their own value. They find ways to ensure they will be noticed. Frequently, this feeling becomes part of their sexuality. It may induce men and women alike to dress in garments that reveal parts of their bodies that other people cover. When this happens, their exhibitionism becomes part of an erotic lifestyle.

People in this chapter have found ways to make sexual self-display part of their daily routine. They integrate it into their work and their social activities. It fulfills a need that most of us feel to some extent. Unlike the rest of us, however, these people recognize the magnitude of that need and find a way to satisfy it without fearing society's judgments.

UNDIES

Dottie is in her mid-twenties and of medium height. Her hair is brown and a couple of shades darker than her eyes. Although she is somewhat plain-looking and a little on the fleshy side, her vivacious smile makes her appear pretty. When we met her in the office in back of the café that she operates, she was dressed only in a beige cotton bra and panties, of material thin enough for us to see dark disks through the bra and a shadowy triangle within the panties.

I hope it doesn't make you uncomfortable for me to be dressed in my working clothes. I only have a few minutes to talk. Then I have to go back to work.

I've been chubby all my life. When I was a kid, it bothered me, and I was always on a diet of some kind to try to take off weight. But by the time I was out of my teens, I began to accept myself for who I was. It was all right that men didn't turn around to look at me when I walked across the beach in a bathing suit. I guess the pleasures of eating made up for not having a terrific figure.

Maybe it was my love of food that got me into the restaurant business, if you can call it that. I know it's only a café. As soon as I was old enough to work, I started waiting tables in this place. Mr. Underwood, who owned it at the time, named it after himself. But in spite of the big sign out front that said UNDERWOOD'S, people around here just called it Undies.

After I started working here, I discovered something interesting.

Even though nobody would give me a second look in a bathing suit, customers always seemed to be trying to sneak a peek down the front of my blouse. I never went without a bra, so that's all they ever got to see, but it sure didn't stop them from looking. I realized that there's a difference between seeing a woman in a bathing suit and seeing her in her underwear. Maybe because it's forbidden.

I also began to realize that I loved that kind of attention. It made me feel very sexy and desirable. There were times I'd be deliberately careless about the buttons on my blouse, leaving the top two open so the guys would be sure to have a view of my bra when I bent over. I even sewed on a few buttons that were a little too small for the button holes, so they'd pop open once in a while, accidentally on purpose.

I really liked working here. It was where I developed my deep friendship with Vera and Mitzi, my two partners. This is a small community, so everybody knows each other. We all went to the same high school, but somehow we never really got to be close until we all started working here. Even though we usually waited tables on different shifts, there were plenty of days or nights when we'd work at the same time. We started hanging out together after hours, and before long we were the best of friends. They were both bridesmaids at my wedding.

After we had been working together for a while, Mr. Underwood decided he was going to sell the place and retire. The three of us talked it over and decided we'd like to try and buy it. He practically had us running it, anyway. Half the time, when we weren't waiting tables, we'd be taking a turn in the kitchen. The menu is simple enough. Just hamburgers, sandwiches, fries, and stuff like that. Most of the profit comes from beer and wine. Pitchers and carafes. Like I said, it's a small community. People like to come in and sit and talk. Sometimes the drinks are just an excuse for socializing.

We pooled our savings and made Mr. Underwood an offer. By that time, we were almost like his family. He agreed to take the little down payment we were able to put together and accept the rest in monthly payments.

At first, not much changed around here, except that we were the owners. We were serving the same meals, pouring the same drinks, and bringing in about the same money. There's quite a bit of tourist traffic through this area, and we always got our fair share of it. Most of the locals divided their business between us and the bar and grill located about half a mile up the road.

Then about a year ago, things started to change. The tourist trade was still the same, but we seemed to be losing a lot of our regulars. The pitchers of beer and carafes of wine just weren't selling the way they used to. We soon found out the reason. The bar had brought in a couple of pool tables. Now the guys could spend their social time with a glass in one hand and a pool cue in the other. They didn't have a reason to come to Undie's anymore.

We were still managing to meet expenses and make our monthly payments to Mr. Underwood, but there wasn't very much left over for us. We were starting to get worried about how we could possibly continue. One evening after closing, Mitzi and Vera and I had a meeting to try to come up with some kind of plan.

Mitzi was in favor of getting a pool table, like the bar had done. But Vera was against it. "They've been there and done that," she said. "We have to come up with some kind of new idea." She said something about a big-screen TV and pay-per-view sports events, but I pointed out that the bar had that already. We were stumped.

I had a thought, but didn't quite know how to put it. Finally, in desperation I just blurted, "The unofficial name of the place is Undies. What if we all wear underwear?"

Vera didn't understand. "Of course, we wear underwear," she said with a giggle. "At least I do. Don't you?"

Mitzi laughed. "I think she means we should work just in our underwear," she said. "Am I right?" When I nodded silently, she added, "I don't know if you're kidding or not, but it's not such a bad idea."

Vera was shocked. "Hey," she said. "This is a respectable café in a respectable town. What do you want to do, turn it into a brothel? I don't think so."

Before I had a chance to respond, Mitzi jumped in. "Helllooo," she sang. "Who said anything about a brothel? What's the difference between panties and a bra or that bikini I've seen you wear on the beach?"

Vera looked doubtful. So I chimed in. "I agree with Mitzi. I think it would put us on the map. Tourists will tell each other about it, and when word gets around the locals will be flocking. There's nothing about it that isn't respectable. My underwear covers a lot more than a bathing suit would. Especially that little yellow one of yours that Mitzi is talking about." Deep down, I knew from my own experience that in the eyes of most men there's a tremendous difference between even the tiniest bikini and the forbidden sight of a woman in panties. But I wasn't saying so. Vera had always been a little on the conservative side, and I didn't want to make the idea harder for her to accept than it already was.

"Think of the money," Mitzi said wistfully. "Right now, there isn't enough of it to keep us in business. But if we try this, I have a feeling we'll be making money hand over fist. We'll be rich in no time." Hearing no response from Vera, she added, "We could try it for a couple of weeks. If it doesn't work out, we can always drop the idea."

That seemed to do it. Vera nodded her head slowly. "Okay," she said hesitantly. "I'll give it a try."

Convincing Vera was only half the battle for me. She and Mitzi are both single. I still had to get my husband to go along with it. That part wasn't easy. At first, he was outraged. He declared that he wasn't going to have his friends and neighbors gawking at his half-naked wife, and that's all there was to it. But I was determined. I used Mitzi's argument about how I wouldn't be showing anything more than I show at the beach. To prove it, I put on a pair of big old granny panties and a heavy-duty double-stitched bra. "Look," I said. "Can you see anything you wouldn't want others to see?" He had to admit that I was pretty well covered. Finally, he said he'd let me give it a try. He even agreed to repaint the sign for us, so that we could officially change the name of our café from Underwood's to Undies.

We closed for a couple of days to make the new concept more dramatic. On the day we reopened, all three of us arrived half an hour earlier than usual to try to get over our nervousness. We stood together in the office making small talk and stealing glances at the clock. Finally, I said, "Well, it's almost time. I'm going to get undressed for work." I guess it was a lame joke, but it was enough to break the ice. Everybody laughed. Without ceremony, I stepped out of my jeans and peeled off my sweater.

I usually wear simple underwear and had to keep it that way so as not to upset my husband. Besides, I think that it's even sexier, because it's so natural. So I wore a white cotton bra and matching full-cut briefs. It felt a little strange to be stripping down in front of my two friends. Even though we had helped each other shop and had shared dressing rooms in stores, there was something quite different about this. For a moment, they seemed to be staring at me.

Mitzi was next. She reached behind her and unzipped the dress she had on, slipping out of it. Her underwear was much more dramatic than mine—red satin. Her ample breasts seemed to overflow the cups of her bra, and the panties were bikini-cut, coming just above her bush. She has a slim but shapely body, and I just knew that the sight of her would bring in lots of business.

The real surprise came when conservative Vera took off her clothes. Under them, she was wearing a see-through lacy black bra with panties that were little more than a G-string. She's a redhead, and her pale skin and freckled breasts were highlighted by the dark lace. The little triangle of cloth barely covered her down below, showing wisps of curling red hair around its edges. Vera's kind of skinny and boyish-looking, but that lingerie turned her into a centerfold queen.

"Ha," I said. "And I thought you were a prude. Did you always have something like that under your uniform?"

She blushed. "I bought them special," she said in a voice that could just barely be heard. "I decided if I'm going to do this, I'm going to do it all the way."

Word must have spread about the new look at Undies, because we did a fantastic business starting from that first day. All of our old customers came back, along with some local folks who had never been in before. It wasn't only men, either. They brought their wives and girlfriends, too. The atmosphere was friendly in a new kind of intimate way. There were plenty of jokes, but nobody ever got out of line, except an occasional tourist. Whenever that happened, there would always be a couple of local guys to straighten them out.

We were making lots of money. For me, though, the excitement I got from having all those people see me in my underwear was worth even more than the increase in income. I guess I never really knew what an exhibitionist I was. I loved knowing that they were coming to look at me and probably talking to their friends about what they saw. I kept it simple, always wearing cotton, like I'm wearing now. But I started buying the kind that was thin enough to almost see through. I noticed the two of you looking at my nipples and bush. That's all right. Don't be embarrassed. I like it.

In fact I liked it so much that I found myself getting so turned on that sometimes I just had to take a break. I'd come back here to the office and close the door so I could be alone. I'd reach inside my panties and touch myself while thinking about the men who had been staring openly at me in the café. Usually, it would only be a few minutes before I would climax. The first couple of times I did that, I immediately changed into a fresh pair of underpants, certain that people would be able to see wetness on the ones I was wearing when I masturbated. After a while, though, I discovered that it turned me on even more to wear the wet ones.

Late one afternoon, I was back here pleasuring myself when the door suddenly opened. I must have forgotten to lock it. Vera was two steps into the room before she realized I was there. When she saw me with my hand in my panties, her mouth fell open. I could feel myself turning red.

She started to laugh. "You too?" she said. "I thought I was the only pervert in the place." With that, she threw herself into a chair and began rubbing herself right through her teeny-weeny G-string. I watched her as I finished doing myself.

Vera must have told Mitzi about it, because the next day Mitzi mentioned it to me and said that she too found it necessary at times to go into the office for relief. After that, we were all quite casual about our self-gratification. We developed a code. One of us would announce to the others, "I have to go check the ice" and head for the back room. If business was slow, one of the other two might say, "I'll help you." Then both would go into the office together and watch each other masturbate, while the third partner took care of customers out front.

We've talked about it and we all admit that waiting tables in our underwear while people stare at us is just about the biggest turn-on we've ever experienced. I never before felt so attractive or so aroused. Men don't seem to mind my excess flesh. In fact, sometimes I think they look more at me in my simple cotton undies than they do at Mitzi in her satin or at Vera in her almost nonexistent lace. Having them look at me and knowing that they are picturing me nude and maybe imagining sex with me keeps me wet and hot all during business hours and long after. How many people do you know that get that much enjoyment out of their work?

Diddling myself in the back room while one of my partners watches makes the whole experience even more exciting. There are times I think I come with special drama, just because I know Mitzi or Vera is seeing it. Most of the time, I keep my panties on while we masturbate together, but on a few occasions, I took them off. Knowing they were seeing me naked as I touched myself usually made my orgasm explosive.

Of course, my husband doesn't know about the back-room sessions, or how excited I am about showing off my body. He certainly isn't complaining. He has a good job himself, but the extra money I bring in makes him real happy.

Whether he knows it or not, he's receiving the benefit of the excitement I get from my exhibitionism. Most nights, I jump all over him the minute I get home from work. Even if he's tired, I manage to do things to get him aroused and to fill him with sexual energy. He's a much richer man than he would be without my work at Undies. A lot happier, too.

PARTY DANCER

At twenty, Lucas has the appearance of a Greek god. He is six-foot-four and muscular, with eyes the color of the Aegean Sea. The chiseled features of his classic face are surrounded by a wreath of blond curls. His fair skin is darkened by the regular use of a tanning bed. Even when he's seated, the movements of his hands and body are lithe and graceful. When we asked if his athletic physique was the result of hard work at a gym, he flashed two rows or perfect white teeth and chuckled.

Except for when I'm working, I hardly ever do anything physical. I like to say I'm a dancer, but really, all I am is a show-off. I never studied dancing or anything like that, just sort of fell into it out of desperation. After high school, I floundered around for a while, going from one odd job to another, glad if I made a dollar or two over minimum wage. There weren't many opportunities in my small midwestern town for a guy with just a high school education and no interest in doing farm labor. So I decided to try my luck in Los Angeles, city of the stars.

Don't get me wrong, I didn't have any plans to get into show business or anything, because I don't have any particular talent. I just figured there would be more opportunities in a big city like that. I bought a bus ticket, kissed my Momma good-bye, and headed for the coast.

It turned out there wasn't much going on in the job market out here, either. I ended up working in a car wash, where I was the only towel slinger who spoke English. That was during the day. I had to look for a second job at night because otherwise I wouldn't have had enough to eat and pay rent, both. So in the evenings, I was one of those guys who sits in a bullet-proof glass booth at a self-service gas station. It scared the hell out me, but it seemed I wasn't qualified for anything else.

Just when I was thinking of giving it up and going back home, I saw an ad in the paper for male dancers at a club. I had heard of the place. It was a strip joint where it was the men who were onstage and the women who shouted, "Take it off!" Ordinarily, I wouldn't have had the nerve, since I had never done anything like dancing. But the ad said, "Experience great but not necessary," and I was desperate. So I thought I'd give it a try.

It said "Apply in person," and there was no phone number, so I just went down there. There must have been a hundred guys applying for the job. The interviews were being held right there in the club. All the tables and chairs had been pushed back against the wall, so we were all standing up, just sort of milling around in a crowd and waiting our turns. There was no real organization. The manager would just step up onstage, point to one of the guys kind of at random, and say, "Let's see what you can do." Then the one who was chosen would get up there and dance to music coming from the sound system.

Most of the guys were prepared with costumes under their clothes. They would gyrate a little and peel their clothes off as they went, usually ending up in a satin thong or G-string. When they were done, the boss just said, "Thank you. Maybe we'll call you."

As I watched six or so guys try out, I started to feel very awkward. They all seemed to know what they were doing, and I sure didn't. Besides, I wasn't at all prepared costume-wise. I think I was getting ready to sneak out when the manager pointed in my direction and said, "You, Apollo. Let's see what you can do."

I looked around to see who Apollo was and then realized he was talking to me. Numbly, I walked up on to the stage. When I got there, I froze. My feet seemed to be glued to the floor and I'm pretty sure my heart stopped beating. What the hell was I supposed to do now? I looked out toward the crowd of guys waiting for their turns, but saw nothing. Suddenly, the voice of Bob Seger filled the room singing "The Fire Down Below." It happened to be one of my favorite songs. I started moving to the beat, like I always do when I hear that tune. Before I knew it, I was gyrating like Mick Jagger and jumping all over the stage.

I remembered what I was there for and started pulling off my clothes. All I had underneath was a pair of white briefs, but I strutted as though it was a star-spangled G-string. I must have been inspired by the music. When it was over and I stopped, some of the guys actually applauded. The boss said, "Put your clothes on and wait for me in the back room," pointing toward the rear of the stage.

That was the beginning of my new career. The club didn't pay much, but the tips were tremendous. I would make more money in one night dancing than I used to make on both my jobs. The club had very strict rules. Never go beyond the G-string—I had to buy a few of those—and never have any contact with the women in the audience, either on or off the premises. But we were allowed to let them tuck dollar bills, and five-dollar bills, and ten-dollar bills, into the waistband of the G-string. Some nights I'd take in two or three hundred dollars.

Honest, I thought I was doing it just for the money. I developed a following and even had a small fan club of women who came back night after night just to see me. I liked that. It gave me a lot of emotional satisfaction to know that they were paying to look at my almost-naked body. I never thought of myself as an exhibitionist, though. I just thought it was the best-paying job I could ever hope to get. For me, it had nothing to do with sex. Or so I thought.

I got a nice apartment. I bought a nice car. I wore good clothes. I even ate in some restaurants that were supposedly frequented by movie stars, although I never really saw one. Well, once, that guy from the TV show. The one about cops in Chicago or someplace. I don't remember the name of it.

One night, I told another one of the dancers at the club that I felt like I was in hog heaven with all the money I was making. He just laughed. This was nothing, he said. If I was interested, he could tell me where the real money was. Well, naturally I was interested. Wouldn't you be?

He told me about dancing at private parties. Swing parties, he said. He said he danced, he ate, he drank, he fucked, and he made a fortune. The hosts or hostesses paid him a big chunk up front, but most of it was tips he got for special favors he gave the men and women there.

I had heard of Hollywood swingers. But, hey, I'm from a small town. I thought I knew what he was talking about, but you don't really know about these things until you really know about them, if you know what I mean. What an eye-opener I had in store for me.

I said I was definitely interested, and he promised to pass my name and number along to someone he knew. A few days later, I got a call and was hired for that very weekend. I wasn't scheduled to work at the club that night anyway. It turned out to be the best thing that ever happened to me, because if I had been on at the club, I probably would have turned down the new job.

When I showed up at the address I was given in the hills, I was blown away. I don't know much about real estate, but I knew that house had to be worth at least ten million. I was greeted at the door by a good-looking, middle-aged blond woman dressed in a real expensive black lace negligée. Hardly worth the trouble, since I could see her tits and big pink nipples right through it. I tried not to stare. After all, I was here for business and couldn't afford to be distracted by sex. Ha. What a dummy I was. And, boy, how much I learned about myself in just that one night.

She led me to a bedroom in the back of the house so the guests wouldn't see me until I was ready to perform. She gave me a drink and told me to get ready. I changed into my dancing clothes while I waited for her to return. I didn't have to wait long. A few minutes later, she was back. Taking me by the hand, she led me into a large living room. The chairs and couches had been placed in a circle to create a dancing area in the center of the floor. It was covered by a carpet so thick that I felt my bare feet sinking into it.

I blinked and looked around. The room was filled with people. They looked like ordinary folks here to see a show. Maybe a little more affluent than I was used to, but not that different from the audiences at the club. Except that there were men as well as women. That was a little strange for me, but what the hell. I knew how to dance so I would dance. I heard a voice shout, "All right, let's see what he's got."

With that the music began to play, and I started to dance. I did my usual thing, stripping my way down to a satin leopard-pattern G-string, until I was moving slowly around in a circle, thrusting my pelvis back and forth. At the club, that would have been the finale, the part when the women started stuffing money into the waistband. But that wasn't happening here. I kept gyrating and dancing until I heard a voice yell, "Take it off already!"

I had been brainwashed by the management at the club to stay strictly within legal bounds. But I suddenly realized that wasn't what I had been hired to do here. A funny thing happened. As soon as I decided to take it all off, I became aroused. That sort of thing never happened at the club, but here I was with a massive hard-on. I felt it pushing against the front of my G-string. As I looked around the room, I realized that all eyes were on it. That made it even stiffer and harder. I was embarrassed about it, but again a voice shouted, "Take it off! Show us what you've got."

What else could I do? As I began peeling the G-string slowly down over my hips, I was sure the boner would go away. After all, I was a professional. Why should this exposure arouse me this way? Surely I'd be soft in a minute. But it seemed to keep getting harder and bigger. I couldn't stall anymore. I pulled down the skimpy garment, which wasn't doing much to cover it anyway, and kicked it off. One of the women got off her couch and picked up the G-string. She started rubbing it against the front of her blouse, across her tits, and down over the crotch of her silk pants. That turned me on even more.

Automatically, I continued gyrating, trying to forget that I was totally naked. It was like trying to forget that you're standing in the middle of a forest fire. I was getting hotter by the minute and, as I moved, my stiff cock was bobbing up and down, pointing at the people who were staring at it. "Nice dick," I heard someone mutter.

Without even knowing what I was doing, I started moving closer to the people sitting in a circle around me, waving my hard-on practically in their faces. Suddenly, one of the women reached out and grabbed it. I kept moving my hips from side to side as she softly pulled it up and down. I heard her moan and I couldn't help moaning back. "Hey, I think he likes it," she said with a laugh.

The man sitting next to her laughed louder and said, "Yeah, and I think you like it too."

Another one of the women shouted, "Don't hog it all to yourself! I want to taste that thing." Before I knew it, she was out of her chair and kneeling on the floor in front of me. In a split second, I felt the warmth of her mouth closing around my swollen cock. It startled me, but boy did it feel good. Especially with all those other people looking on. A man who was obviously her husband got up and stood behind her. Putting his hands on her shoulders, he murmured, "Yes, suck it. Suck his big cock."

I had never experienced anything like this before. It was like losing my virginity all over again. It was the most exciting moment of my life. There were at least a dozen people cheering as I stood naked in their midst receiving a world-class blowjob from a woman I didn't even know, while her husband urged her on. I looked around and knew that as much as it was turning me on, it was turning the audience on as well. That turned me on even more.

It was my show, so I took command. Reaching down, I tangled my fingers in her hair and pulled her gently away from my cock. There were other women in the room, and I was sure they all wanted a piece of me. I was right. When I sidestepped to the left, there was another woman waiting to take her place. I grabbed this one by the hair and pulled her forward, driving my cock into her open mouth. Her mate played with her tits as her tongue moved expertly over the head of my cock. I gave her a couple of minutes and moved on.

For at least half an hour, I shared my swollen cock with woman after woman, and even man after man. Finally, when I was sure I just couldn't hold it anymore, I pulled back and stroked it with my own hand. One of the women, sensing what was about to happen, tore open her blouse and pulled down her bra. When I started to come, I aimed it at her tits and let it fly all over her. As I covered her nipples with my hot semen her husband slipped a couple of bills into my hand.

Later, I discovered that he had given me two hundred dollars. Other men and women handed me money too. When I was totally spent, the hostess led me back to the bedroom where I started out. Alone, I counted the money and found that I had received close to a thousand dollars.

The night wasn't over. A little while later, the hostess returned and asked if I was ready for another performance. I sure was. In fact, my cock had been hard again just minutes after coming. The whole idea of being on sexual display was like an aphrodisiac. This time, I started out naked and just gyrated around the circle stroking my cock and waving it at the audience, or bending over and spreading my ass cheeks so they could look between my legs from behind. By now, most of people in the room were naked too. Some were screwing, looking up at me to make themselves hotter while I performed for them. When my performance reached its climax, one of the women bent over for me to fuck her from behind while everyone watched and cheered.

Never before had I felt so vibrant or so aware of who I was and what my life was all about. The sex was great, but the best part was the way the crowd reacted to my nudity and to my erotic antics. By the end of the night, I had taken in close to fifteen hundred dollars. The hostess assured me she would want me to return. She explained that each couple in the group took a turn hosting the par-

ties and said she was sure that others would be requesting my services, too.

I've worked those swing parties regularly ever since. I'm rolling in
money and living the good life. But I'm going to tell you something.
I'd do it for free if I had to. Who would have thought that sweet
young Lucas from a small town in America's heartland turns out to
be the world's greatest exhibitionist? The thrill I get from being on
sexual display is something I can't even begin to describe. Maybe
you can in that book of yours.

2
THE MORE
THE
MERRIER

SOME PEOPLE FEEL THAT THE STRUCTURE OF CONVEN- tional sexual morality in our society is calculated to frustrate them by severely restricting their choice of sex partners. Until recently, laws against homosexuality closed everyone's bedroom door to half the world's population. The tenets of many religions still do. Other regulations prohibit sex with someone who is married to another, or with someone who is not married to anybody at all. The only legitimate choice is one's own spouse.

Limiting sexual contact to one person throughout life carries the advantage of permitting partners to learn each other's likes and dislikes so they can adapt themselves accordingly. It also carries the disadvantage of making sexuality lackluster or even boring, however. Divorce is one way to avoid the monotony of monogamy. Another is adultery. Either option can lead to heartache.

The people whose stories are told in this chapter found an alternative. After their initial experiments with multiple-partner sex were successful, they made it the solution to problems that otherwise might have hurled their marriages onto the rocks of disaster. Dirk and Sally found a way of satisfying a need for variety that they both felt, although Sally was probably not aware of it until Dirk introduced her to a different way of life. Rosemary and Jay had dark desires that each kept hidden from the other until they discovered that both could be fulfilled by bringing a third person into their bedroom. Although the activities comprising their erotic lifestyles are not identical, both couples engage in some form of group eroticism on a regular basis.

OUR WONDERFUL THREE-WAYS

Rosemary is a young twenty-nine who says she feels more like eighteen. Her hair is bright red and comes down to the middle of her back. She has beautiful dark brown eyes that are almond-shaped with long red lashes that touch her red eyebrows. Her skin is creamy white and splattered with lots of freckles all over her high cheekbones. She is of medium height with a body that fits her physique perfectly—not at all overweight, and not too thin. She dresses like a teenager in tight-fitting and revealing outfits. Her nails are manicured and polished in bright red to match what she is wearing. Rosemary loves to talk and isn't at all inhibited when we ask intimate questions about her erotic lifestyle.

I work as a waitress in a chic Los Angeles restaurant. There's a Hollywood joke that says, "Oh, you're an actor. What restaurant?" And it's true. Most of the waiters and waitresses I work with want to become movie stars. They all get small parts occasionally, but make their living at the restaurant. I seem to be the only one there without great ambitions and aspirations to become the next Hollywood sensation. The rest of them are always hoping that they will be discovered with a tray of dishes in their hand when some movie director or agent spots them.

It's the kind of restaurant where something like that could happen. Lots of motion picture moguls come in to eat and to see and be seen. I like working there. The nice thing about people who are hoping to become the next Mel Gibson or Julia Roberts is that most of them are beautiful and charming people. They are all friendly and never at a loss for conversation. Sometimes, they get the inside dope on those movieland scandals you see on TV. Hearing all their tales and gossip makes my job even more interesting.

I was working here before I got married a couple of years ago and continued after Jay and I tied the knot. The tips are great, and heaven knows we can use the money. The best thing about my job is that it gives me the opportunity to experience the kind of sex that I always dreamed of.

Ever since puberty, I spent many hours a day thinking about sex. If I had spent as much time on my studies as I did daydreaming of sex, I wouldn't be waiting tables today. The thing I fantasized about the most was having two men at the same time. I never told my husband about my fantasy, because I was sure he'd never understand. Many times during intercourse, I thought of telling him about these thoughts that turn me on, but always decided that I'd better not go there. I was certain it was no more than a secret fantasy that I'd spend my life wondering about and keeping to myself.

Jay is a wonderful lover and is always ready to excite me. There is nothing that he wouldn't do to please me sexually. Our lovemaking is always fulfilling. Somewhere deep inside me, though, I was aware that there's a difference between fulfillment and over-the-top fulfillment. So as I was being fulfilled, I was dreaming of the ultimate— two guys fucking me and pleasing my body at the same time. Just thinking about it kept me excited and stimulated, but it also left me feeling a wee bit disappointed with even the most satisfying sex with Jay. Maybe I was especially ready when Sammy and I had that conversation on that fateful day.

Sammy was a fairly new waiter at the restaurant. Man, was he good-looking. He had the kind of charisma that could make him a leading man in the movies and was blessed with the sort of charm that knocks your socks off. He was so handsome that he was almost pretty. When we were working together, I couldn't tear my eyes off of him. He started coming on to me the minute he began working there, but in a friendly, flirtatious way that I could take seriously if I wanted to, or just accept as banter if I did not.

That was how I decided to see it, at first. When he'd proposition me, I would just laugh and flirt back a little. I guess that encouraged him, because he kept it up and kept it up. He was a few years younger than me, and that was kind of nice. After all, what woman wouldn't feel good about a younger man coming on to her? He was always telling me what great sex we could have. I just let it go in one ear and out the other.

Then one day my husband came into the restaurant to drop off my car keys. Sammy and I were on break at the time. After Jay left, Sammy said in his half joking, half serious way that the three of us should get it on one night. I realized the idea of that had always been a wish inside me, but still I couldn't take him seriously. So I just laughed. Sammy wouldn't let me off the hook that easily, though. "Wouldn't you like to feel me and Jay doing you at the same time?" he whispered, simulating a hoarse voice.

"Look," I snapped. "My husband would never consider anything like that and it just won't happen." I guess subconsciously I was letting him know that I liked the idea and that Jay was the only obstacle to it.

That was when Sammy dropped the bomb. "Jay would love it," he said. "Don't you know your husband is bi?"

I gasped with shock. "How can you say such a thing, Sammy? Nobody knows Jay like I do. He's my husband. You're absolutely wrong."

Sammy wouldn't let it drop. Persistently he insisted, "Why don't you just suggest it to him and see what he says. I'll bet you anything that he goes for it. When he does, you'll know I'm right. I'll tell you what: If you really put it to him and he hates the idea, like you think he will, I promise I'll never bring it up again."

I just waved my hand angrily to shoo away his ridiculous notion.

All the rest of that day, though, I couldn't stop thinking about what he said. Could Jay really be bisexual? It's not the kind of thing a man would be likely to tell his wife, so maybe it was true. The more I thought about it, the more I started to agree with Sammy. I had noticed that Jay seemed to be checking out the handsome waiters every time he came into the restaurant. At the beach, he never missed an opportunity to comment on all the good-looking guys in tight-fitting bathing suits. Sometimes he'd even point out the way the Speedos showed off a man's package, which was what Jay called his cock and balls.

One night, as Jay and I were having sex, I just blurted it out. "What if there was another man with us?" I whispered. With that, Jay started to come inside me and the air was filled with the sounds of his orgasm. For a few minutes after that there was silence. Afterwards, Jay looked at me in a bewildered sort of way and didn't say a word. I wasn't even sure he had heard what I said. Then, tentatively, he asked, "Is that something you would want?"

He sounded interested, but I was afraid to let him know how I really felt. So I just murmured, "If you'd like to try something like that."

"I could get into it," he replied. "If you could." We talked about it quietly for a while, both of us slowly realizing that we were serious, that it was something that could actually happen. I got the feeling he had been dreaming about it as long as I. At one point, he said, "Oh, but who could we get?"

I jumped at the opportunity. "Do you know Sammy, the waiter at the restaurant? I'm pretty sure he'd be interested in something like that."

Jay tried to sound casual when he said, "Sammy? Oh, yeah, I think I know which one he is. Well, I guess you could ask him." I could tell by the tension in his throat that he remembered very well who Sammy was and was struggling not to show his excitement.

For a moment, I found myself wondering, almost angrily, whether he was interested in doing this for my pleasure, or because he wanted to have sex with Sammy as much as I did. Then I realized that it didn't make any difference. Either way, the idea of that threesome was tremendously exciting. I think the talk Jay and I had that night was the beginning of a new erotic lifestyle for both of us. I would no longer have to wonder what it would be like to fuck two men at the same time, because the fantasy was about to become a reality.

Sammy wasn't at all surprised when I told him that Jay bought the idea and was willing to give it a try. He just flashed a knowing smile. Sammy admitted that he found Jay attractive, too. After that, every move he made while waiting tables and every look he gave me reminded me that the three of us were going to get together for sex. Work became a kind of foreplay.

A few days later, Sammy came back to our house with me after work. Jay was waiting, and the three of us shared a couple of bottles of wine so we could be more relaxed. Jay and Sammy took the opportunity to get better acquainted. I was beginning to wonder how this thing would ever start rolling.

Finally, Sammy took the initiative. In that casual manner of his, he got up from the couch and began undressing. Jay and I watched in silence, until not a stitch of clothes covered his body. I was becoming very excited thinking about what was about to happen. The sight of Sammy's erection had me wet. I glanced over at Jay to check out his reaction.

He was staring openly at Sammy's nakedness. I could see from the expression on his face that he was most definitely aroused. Sammy's body is lean but in great shape. With his aspirations to stardom, he worked hard at his appearance. Jay was looking at him the way he sometimes looks at me. I couldn't help but notice that Sammy seemed equally interested in Jay.

While I was thinking about all this, Jay stood up and quickly undressed. Now I was the only one with clothes on. It made me nervous and a little uncomfortable to think that both of them would have nothing to do but watch me as I stripped. But I was mistaken about that.

As I got up and began removing my clothes, I realized neither of them was even looking in my direction. That made it a little easier. Sammy and Jay were feasting their eyes on each other's naked bodies. Both had tremendous hard-ons. They just stood there in the center of the room, staring at each other's erections. As I removed the last garment from my body, Jay just glanced at me and suggested that we go to the bedroom.

When the three of us were standing nude around the bed, I decided not to take the initiative and waited for further instructions from the men. Sammy placed himself in charge. "Why don't you lie on the bed," he whispered, talking to me, but still staring at Jay. "So your husband and I can properly seduce you." I looked at Jay, who was nodding his agreement. This was it. I was finally going to realize my dream.

As I positioned my naked body onto the bed, my heart was pounding with excitement. I was about to be stroked and petted by two men at the same time. My nipples ached as they grew larger and harder.

With my back against the mattress, I looked at my two lovers. Standing by the foot of the bed, Jay took my ankles in his hand and spread them slowly apart. This gave him and Sammy a full view between my legs and into my pussy. Sammy moved toward my head and began running his fingers slowly up and down my shoulders and down my arms. I started to feel little goose bumps all over my skin. Jay was stroking my legs lightly with his fingertips until they reached up to my inner thighs. What a tingling effect all this petting was having on my body. My sensations were building.

I could feel my nipples getting harder even though they had not yet been touched. I reached out and took hold of each of their cocks in one of my hands. They were vibrating in the air demanding my attention, but still I couldn't believe that I had enough nerve to get down to the nitty-gritty that way. Their cocks were so big and beautiful, and when I touched the soft smooth skin of their two shafts, I felt them grow even harder. I moved my hands up and down on two cocks simultaneously and loved every second of it.

Sammy's hands were now playing with my breasts. I could feel his fingers massaging and kneading the soft skin of my tits, while my nipples became as erect as their hard-ons. Each second brought greater and greater excitement to me, while I felt the pleasures coursing through my body. I thrilled to the knowledge that I was holding two cocks at the same time. I could hear satisfaction coming from their throats and could feel their bodies rocking to my masturbating touch.

Jay's fingers were moving in on my vagina, and I gasped with anticipation. I was so hot that the inside of my pussy was spouting with fluid. The deeper his finger surged inside, the more I oozed. The lips of my vagina spread open like a budding flower. I quivered with a thrilling passion as Jay's finger worked its magic. At first, his finger explored the walls of my pussy, feeling every crevice. He explored the sensitive membranes that lined my sex. When I felt his finger plunge deep inside me at the same moment that Sammy began gently twisting my swollen nipples, my whole body trembled from all the wonderful sensations.

I couldn't believe how quickly an orgasm was building inside me. It usually took me a long time to come. Sometimes, when Jay and I were fucking, it would take so long that I'd pretend to come, just so we could stop. But now I rose fast, feeling a sexual high that took my breath away. Having two lovers touching and feeling me at the same time as I touched both of them was more than I could bear. Before I knew what hit me, I started to orgasm. I felt like I had left my body and gone to paradise.

When I started to come back and return to normal, my hands let go of my lovers. I was so exhausted by my new out-of-body experience that I had to take a moment to catch my breath. I closed my eyes. When I opened them, my husband and Sammy were playing with each other's cocks. Sammy's face had a look of passion written all over it, and Jay showed no inhibitions as he worked on Sammy's hard-on. The two guys were enthralled with one another. I watched to see who would be the first to come.

Both men were actively involved with giving and receiving a hand-job. Their bodies rocked, every movement seeming to ripple through their throbbing cocks. It didn't take long before Jay was shooting a whirling load. Sammy immediately followed. I couldn't believe the facial expression on my husband's face when Sammy brought him to climax. It was absolutely thrilling to watch my husband's passions being fulfilled by a man who had just helped fulfill mine.

After we had time to rest and settle down, our sex play started all over again. By the time our evening was over, I couldn't think of anything, or any position, or any possibility that we didn't try. Our sex orgy lasted for several hours, and when none of us could possibly go another round, we called it a night. That was the beginning of many more two-man–one-woman sexual encounters. It feels great to be that woman.

Jay and I have learned to be perfectly honest with each other. We share other men regularly, now. I think it has brought our marriage to a new level of sexual bliss. If not for our experience with Sammy, we might have kept secret from each other our most fervent sexual desires. I might never have told Jay how I longed to be with two men at the same time. He might never have told me how he craves the touch of another man. Now that we truly know each other, we see that our sexual desires are incredibly compatible.

Waitressing is a wonderful way for me to meet new partners who are willing to join me and my husband for the kind of sex we all want. For some reason, Hollywood seems to draw bisexual men. I'll admit that at first it bothered me a little that Jay can get even more turned on by another man than he does with me alone. But it doesn't trouble me at all anymore. Since this started, I've met lots of men who like having sex with both genders. I've even come across some who left their wives to run off with another guy.

Because of our new erotic lifestyle, both of us are satisfied. Jay won't have to leave me to fuck other men. And my desire for two men at once won't turn me against him. What could have been a negative in our relationship has turned into a positive. We can share the enjoyment of our sexual preferences together and live happily ever after.

COUPLES' MASSAGE WORKSHOP

Dirk is thirty-six years old and is a mountain of a man. He is very tall, at least six-foot-six, and could easily play the role of Hercules in a motion picture epic. Everything about him is large—bulging muscles, expansive chest, and huge hands. Even his brown eyes are big, as is the smile that seems to stretch from ear to ear. His hair is very light blond, the color that many women get from peroxide. There is a long scar that runs from one side of his forehead to the other, the souvenir of what he calls his first and last ski trip. He has a warm and friendly personality and is obviously a man who enjoys the company of others.

You've got to promise me that when you print this, you're going to disguise us real well. I think if people knew up front what my wife Sally and I are thinking when they come to our workshops, a lot of them might not come. Once they get into it with us, everything is just fine. But most of them would never get that far if they couldn't tell themselves in advance that all they're after is an educational experience. Well, maybe I'm getting a little ahead of my story. So, like the man said, let me begin at the beginning.

Sex is very important to me. I've always felt it was all right to do whatever it took to fulfill my needs, as long as nobody gets hurt along the way. Problem is that the first time around I was the one who got hurt. I guess that's okay, though. I learned from bitter experience.

When I was younger, I felt differently about things than I do now. I used to go to wild sex parties and throw all caution to the wind. I met my first wife at one of those parties. A friend of mine brought me along to the home of someone he knew. There was lots of drinking and dope-smoking, and before long everyone there was running around naked and screwing anybody they happened to bump into.

A sexy lady named Doris jumped my bones soon after the festivities began. She practically raped me. Well, maybe "rape" isn't the right word, since I certainly was not resisting her. What a body she had. Tits the size of balloons and a split-melon ass every man dreams about.

Man, what a sexual appetite that Doris had. I pounded her pussy the way only a young stud can. As soon as we were done, she was up and ready to fuck someone else. I found another willing partner, and another after that. But I kept my eyes on Doris all night. As soon as I saw her alone, I grabbed her for some more hot fucking. How could I help it? I fell in love with her and asked her to marry me that same night.

She just laughed. It was all a joke to her. I was persistent. I called her. I took her to dinner. I let her take me to a few more sex parties. I asked her to marry me every chance I got. Finally she consented. Oh, it was great. Well, I mean while it lasted. We had hot sex day and night. We continued going to parties where we would freely exchange partners and have group sex left and right.

I was proud of the fact that our relationship was open. It was okay with me for her to fuck every other guy in sight, because I knew I was the one she had married. I even enjoyed watching her fuck other men. After all, that was only recreation. I was the one she loved. I was the one she came home to. Boy, was I in for a surprise. She ended up running off with one of those men I had watched her fucking. We were divorced less than a year after we were married. I heard she's been married seven or eight times since then.

I decided it was the loose lifestyle that had caused the problem. She had fucked me without even knowing my name and married me soon afterwards. It was inevitable that she'd end up feeling the same way about other guys she fucked. My mistake was in being so free and easy about all that swapping and switching and group sexing. I resolved not to make the same mistake again.

Sally, my second wife . . . well, I mean my present wife . . . well, I mean my wife forever . . . she never was into that free and easy sex. I wasn't her first, of course. When I met her, she'd been with her share of men. But she was conventional. One partner at a time. No outside fooling around.

I was honest with her about my background. It didn't bother her that I had been in an open marriage or that I had gone to sex parties where everybody fucked everybody else. That was the past. She was willing to trust me, but she made it clear from the start that she had no interest in fucking other men and wouldn't want me to be fucking other women. I was glad, because I could at least be sure I'm not going to lose her to some guy I've swapped mates with for the evening.

After a while, I found myself missing the sexual variety that comes with swinging. I think I came up with a perfect solution, though. Well, I mean the workshops I was telling you about. Let me explain.

Before we met, Sally had taken some courses in massage. After we got married, she bought a folding massage table and gave me the best massages I ever had in my life. She has a real talent for it. She used her hands to bring me total relaxation. Then, after half an hour or so, she'd turn it into a hot sexual experience for me.

She'd use the tips of her fingers to stroke my whole body till I was tingling with desire. Then she'd concentrate on the most sensitive spots—my nipples, the insides of my thighs, my ass, my scrotum, and finally my cock. She'd touch me so lightly that it felt like a feather. I'd just drift off with my eyes closed, basking in the wonderful sensation. When I thought I was feeling as good as a person can possibly feel, she'd take my cock in her mouth and finish me off with a long, slow, tantalizing blowjob until I went off like a Roman candle.

Naturally, I wanted to be able to return the favor. So I asked her to teach me some of what she had learned about massage. She did. I was clumsy at first, but I got better at it with practice. She would lie passive on the table while I stroked and petted her. I learned to find all her sensitive spots and make the most of them with my fingers and mouth.

After a while, I signed up for some classes at a massage school. She did too. We decided to take the full course and get massage licenses. We had no idea what we were ever going to do with them, but figured that we might as well go for it. Well, I mean we were going to the massage school anyway. It turned out to be a great idea.

We kept learning new things and practicing our techniques until we learned to keep each other on the brink of climax for hours at a time. It was wonderful to be the receiver and just as great to be the giver. Our sex was superb.

But something was missing. Well, I mean I missed the sexual variety I had known before meeting Sally. I began to think that we might both find greater satisfaction if we could bring others into our massage-play. At the massage school, all the students in the class would take turns massaging each other under the instructor's supervision. Of course, there was no sex involved. But it became perfectly natural for us to be touching other naked people and to be naked while other people were touching us. The sheets we used to drape ourselves with didn't really cover much, and they had a tendency to slip off during the massage. So Sally had become comfortable with being naked and touched by strangers, and equally comfortable with touching naked strangers.

Still, I hesitated to mention the idea of bringing others into our home sex-massage games. When I finally did, she hesitated to respond. But I could see that the idea had some appeal for her. Finally she agreed to give it a try, but only with people we didn't know. I posted a few vaguely worded notices on the Internet and established telephone contact with an interested couple within a few days. On the phone, we were all very frank about the idea that it would be an erotic thing and that it would be experimental. Well, I mean we agreed that anyone could decide to stop at any time. I think that made it easier for Sally.

That weekend, the four of us got together at our house. Ava and Luke were a young unmarried couple who were interested in experiencing a wide variety of sexual pleasures. After the introductions and small talk, we all undressed. It was a little awkward for Sally. At the massage school, we would undress behind a curtain and wrap ourselves in a sheet before getting onto the tables. Here, we were all in the same room, quite openly watching each other taking our clothes off. Sally was game, though. I found it very exciting to see her strip in front of the others. By the time she was naked, my cock was hard. I saw Ava glance at it, and that made it even more erect.

Ava's tits were not huge, but they were ample. Her ass was large but firm. I'd have to say that she was definitely on the meaty side. Well, I mean she was extremely sensual. Her bush was like a jungle. Some guys like them shaved, but I prefer them hairy. Sally trims hers for bikinis, even though I've asked her not to. Seeing Ava's growing wild was a real treat for me. It reminded me how much I had been missing sexual variety.

Ava jumped at the chance to be first on the table. She lay there with her back against the cushioned surface, completely exposed to our gazing eyes while each of us privately assessed her nude body. Her tits stood straight up, and her little nipples were beginning to bud. Her boyfriend, Luke, stood by, not quite knowing what to do and waiting for one of us to direct him. Sally stood by Ava's head. I positioned myself in the middle of the table. Finally, I gestured for Luke to go to the foot end.

Sally set the pace. She began to rub oil on Ava's shoulders and arms, working very slowly, making sure that she didn't miss any skin. Luke picked up the bottle of oil and began to apply it from her toes to her knees. I worked her body from the knees up. I began coating her thighs with oil, kneading it deeply into her skin. Ava was feeling six hands at once. Well, I mean thirty fingers were kneading and massaging her body, all at the same time.

Ava kept her eyes closed most of the time, showing us the pleasure she was feeling. Whenever she opened them, she'd look at each of us in turn, watching what we were doing. Sally was approaching her upper torso and oiling her upper chest. At the massage school, there had never been any touching of breasts, so I wondered what my pretty wife was going to do. I watched as her hands worked their way slowly to Ava's breasts. Then, before my eyes, Sally drizzled some oil on them and began to spread the oil evenly with her fingers.

Ava made a sound of sexual bliss. I could see her nipples growing harder and more erect. I thought this might discourage Sally, but I was much mistaken. As Ava's swollen buds grew, my wife busied her fingers stroking all around them. I had felt her hands massaging my nipples many times and had a pretty good idea of what Ava was feeling. My cock was jumping up and down, half hidden by the table as I watched my wife pluck and tweak the other woman's nips.

Luke and I were rubbing Ava while we watched Sally's hands give fulfillment to her breasts. Slowly and methodically, she stroked and manipulated Ava's tits until every drop of oil had been thoroughly absorbed by the palpitating flesh. It was fascinating to watch one woman, my wife, giving pleasure to another, Luke's girlfriend.

By now, I was coating Ava's abdomen with the oil, spreading it all over her belly. My fingers could feel her body responding to the pleasures the three of us were giving her. Her legs were parting gradually. I moved my hands to one of her inner thighs, while her boyfriend stroked the other. Our hands worked gently, and with each stroke her legs spread a little wider. I could see the inside of her pussy as she opened herself up.

I teased her body, moving up the length of her leg to come within a hair's breadth of her pink pussy. She was panting with desire to be touched where she wanted it most. Her body was relaxed, but suffused with the kind of sexual tension that operates below the surface. She was moaning softly, letting us all know that we were giving her pleasure.

Sally's fingers rolled and twisted Ava's nipples, tweaking gently to bring the panting woman's passions to a higher level. My eyes moved from Ava's moistening pussy to her heaving breasts, where my wife skillfully stroked her. My cock was stirring mightily. Well, I mean to tell you the truth, I never thought my wife would be so good at playing with another woman's nipples. I could see that she was enjoying this as much as I, because Sally's own nipples were erect and darkening in color.

Luke's eyes were shifting from Sally's tits to her hands on Ava's nipples. I noticed that he too had a mammoth hard-on. He had gone back to playing with his girlfriend's toes, leaving her pussy to me. He was taking his time, twisting and pulling gently on each individual toe. He seemed to know a little bit about massage himself.

My hands were working their way toward her slit, teasing her occasionally by brushing lightly over the lips of her pussy. Ava's pelvis rocked, as though begging and pleading for my fingers to touch the inside of her womanhood. Every few seconds her eyes would open, looking at me beseechingly. I controlled myself, holding off until I couldn't stand it any longer. Then I began to freely touch and pet her pubic mound.

I pulled softly at her thick pubes and twirled strands of the coarse hair around my fingers. Then, with a teasing circular motion, I pressed the palm of my hand gently against her mound. I could hear her gasping cries of pleasure as she accepted my touch. Then, slowly, very slowly, my fingers pulled the lips of her vulva apart and I paused to look inside. The color of her inner lips was a deep red, and they were coated with a shiny liquid that made them appear even brighter. I held her open wide, making sure that Luke had every opportunity to look inside and to see his girlfriend's pussy being handled by another man. Well, I mean I'd been there with Doris, and I know how exciting that can be.

As Sally pleasured Ava's nipples and Luke worked his fingers up her legs, I began to slip my finger inside her. It glided in without the slightest bit of effort. She was as hot and wet as a swamp in there. I could almost imagine steam wafting from her writhing opening. I started to explore the cavern of her pussy, touching and feeling the consistency of her lubricated tissues. I had two, and then three fingers inside, twisting them and turning them, while her boyfriend watched me plundering her.

Sally was watching me too, and from the look on her face, I could see that the scene was turning her on. That made me even hotter. Getting my wife stimulated this way was like the thrill of a lifetime. I loved knowing that she and I were both bringing sexual pleasure to another woman. I loved the idea that each of us would soon be taking a turn on the table.

Ava's big clit was poking its way out from its nest. It was huge, the size of a bing cherry, and almost purple in color. I had been with lots of women, but had never seen such an enormous clit. I had an over-powering urge to taste it while my wife looked on. Without another moment's hesitation, I bent down, stuck my tongue out, and started to explore it. It had a tantalizing, spicy flavor that made my whole mouth tingle. I rolled my tongue all around its entirety, coating it thoroughly with my saliva. I couldn't believe it could get any bigger, but the more I licked it, the larger it grew. Ava was writhing like a wild woman, every part of her body properly tended to.

I looked deliberately at Sally as I licked Ava's clit. The expression on her face was passionate, more aroused than I had ever seen her. Well, I mean I had been surprised to see her getting off playing with Ava's nipples, but it was even more of a surprise to see how excited it was making her to watch me eat the other woman's pussy. My cock was bursting with a wave of electric current that zapped me to a point within inches from a peak.

Ava's body began to tremble. Then she tightened, stiffening on the table. Finally, her hips began whipping up and down as she shouted, "I'm climaxing. Luke, it's happening." She screamed unintelligible sounds as, with an explosive blast, she gushed a river over my tongue. I could feel the fluids overflowing her pussy and covering my chin, while her fingers dug deep into my scalp. Her body shook vio-lently until the surges of her orgasm slowed and every last drop of her fulfillment was spent. When I felt her hands pushing my head away from her, I stopped and moved back.

Ava got up from the table quickly and practically pushed Luke into her place. I mean, it was as though she wanted him to experi-ence some of the ecstasy that had just melted her down. Sally and I quickly changed places. Luke lay on his back, his cock stiff and hard as a bone. It was sticking straight up in the air. From the gleam in Sally's eyes, I could tell that she couldn't wait to get her hands on it. I wanted so much to see her do so.

Ava began immediately to pour oil on Luke's feet and start massaging them. I dripped oil on his arms and shoulders, smoothing the greasy liquid into his skin with deep, heavy strokes. He lay there contentedly, absorbing all the pleasures that were coming his way.

Sally wasted no time. Without preliminary, she took hold of his hard-on and moved it up and down in the palm of her hand. With her other oil-coated hand, she cupped and cuddled his scrotum. He was already starting to stir in response to her expert stroking. At first Sally moved slowly, working heated oil up and down the length of his swollen dick. Gradually, her movements quickened. With each pass of her hand, the color of his cock's head darkened. The veins that ran the length of his shaft started to bulge, until they looked like they were protruding through the thin skin of his penis.

Ava's hands were stroking his inner thighs, and I was oiling his nipples, pinching gently and pulling on them, giving a little twist to each movement. He responded to the six hands that were stimulating him by thrusting his body about on the table. Meaningless nonsense words babbled and bubbled from his lips.

Luke's body was being attended to in every possible sexual way. The faraway look on his face told all of us that he was loving it. Sally's nipples were as hard as ever, as she continued to masturbate his cock, knowing that her husband was watching with approval and excitement. Ava's nipples were starting to bud again as she stroked his thighs. She seemed entranced by the sight of Sally and me giving pleasure to her boyfriend. I knew, and so did Sally, that the best was yet to come for us.

Looking at me, the way I had looked at her, Sally began to lick at Luke's cockhead. She took her time, running her tongue slowly over the swelling knob and around its rim until it was bulging blue. Staring right into my eyes, Sally took the head of his cock into her mouth, swallowing it up until most of the shaft was buried deep inside and away from our sight. Well, I mean what a moment that was.

Ava released a long languid sigh of disbelief. My cock was twitching as I watched my wife do to another man what I knew she did so well. She was using her mouth on him in the way she used it on me. It was thrilling.

Luke was going wild. His body moved up and down. His ass

pushed hard against the massage table so that he had more power to thrust his pelvis up and drive his cock even deeper into Sally's mouth. Sally was sucking him fast and furiously.

I heard Ava gasp as she knew what was about to happen. Within moments, Luke's body began to convulse. He thrashed and bucked as blast after blast of his semen filled my wife's sucking mouth. Sally never stopped sucking his hard-on, keeping it buried deep inside her throat. Even as Luke's movements began to slow down, his cries of orgasmic relief were still issuing from his lips.

When Luke was finished, Sally climbed onto the table. We all made sure to give her the same satisfaction the others had received. Then I had my turn. After Sally's hand pressed my cock against Ava's nipples and I had pumped my juice over Ava's tits, Ava returned to the table. Each of us had several turns as the focus of sexual attention. By the time the evening was over, all four of us had our fill of satisfying sex. After Ava and Luke left, Sally and I fucked for an hour, whispering in each other's ear about the evening's delights.

We found a few other couples the same way we had found Ava and Luke. It was a perfect compromise between swinging and monogamy. Neither of us had actual intercourse with anyone else, and the massage setting kept it light and casual. But it allowed us to experience some kind of sex with other people. The Internet did not seem a reliable enough way of assuring that we would be able to keep playing our newly created game, though.

That was when I came up with the idea of conducting couples' massage workshops. Well, I mean we were both licensed massage therapists. Why not advertise openly and increase the pool of people from whom we could choose? I spoke to a lawyer who took care of the necessary formalities. He even set up a corporation for us. We were in business.

We offer a four-hour workshop in which we agree to teach a couple the art of erotic pleasure-massage. It's perfectly legitimate. We spend about half an hour demonstrating on each other, having the two attendees work on each of us while the other one of us supervises.

Then we have each of them take a turn on the table, while his or her mate joins Sally and me in giving pleasure. Then Sally and I each take a turn on the table so the other two can practice what we've taught them. It isn't always as good as it was that first time with Ava and Luke—but lots of times it's better.

The best part is that we've had a tremendous response to our advertising and an even bigger word-of-mouth response. So we actually have more couples than we have time for. Sally and I know that we can have wonderful touchy, feely, licky, sucky sex experiences with others as often as we want. We are both very happy with our erotic lifestyle and expect it to continue for a very long time. Here, take one of our cards and give us a call sometime if you'd like to try it yourselves.

3
THE THRILL
OF MONEY

WE TEND TO USE THE WORD "PROFESSIONAL" WHEN talking about a doctor or lawyer or member of some other learned occupation. In its most basic sense, however, a professional is anyone who gets paid for what she or he does, as opposed to an amateur, who does it for fun. The word has taken on another meaning, though, one that is even more significant for the people whose stories are told in this chapter. Frequently, it is used to describe a person who is excellent at something, as in saying "He cooks like a professional" or "She's a pro at arranging flowers." So an equation has developed between financial remuneration and outstanding ability.

For some people, this connection between payment for services and superior performance adds a special thrill to sex. Often, those who are paid for sex are classed with the lowest groups in society. There are others, though, who think that receiving money for performing erotic acts places them among an elite group of professionals. To them, payment is evidence of their exceptional talent and skill.

Christopher is a lawyer. Patti calls herself a housewife. On the surface, they have very little in common. One trait they share is the special excitement they receive when a stranger gives them cash for sexual services.

Patti says the money is important not for what it buys, but for the emotion it inspires in her when she receives it. She says it makes her feel sexy and proves that she is a woman. Christopher calls payment a tangible symbol of his sexual success, a badge of his self-worth. In this way, their erotic lifestyles are remarkably similar.

GIGOLO AT LAW

Christopher is the picture of the successful young lawyer. At thirty-three years of age, he wears finely tailored suits and has his dark wavy hair cut by one of the city's best-known stylists. His intelligent brown eyes return the glance of the person with whom he is speaking, indicating complete attention. He is of medium height and carries himself with erect confidence, his back straight, his broad shoulders squared. His smile comes easily but is controlled, as are the movements of his manicured hands, which he uses sparingly to emphasize what he is saying. We are with him in his wood-paneled office as he tells us his rather surprising story.

I studied hard in law school because I knew that the big-money firms would be looking at grades when recruitment time came. Before I graduated, I had five or six offers to choose from. I didn't go for the biggest salary. Instead, I went with the firm that offered the best prospects for partnership. It was the right decision. I became a partner within four years, something of a record around here. Now I'm making much more than I would have at any of the other firms. I specialize in estate planning, and all my clients are quite wealthy. I wouldn't have it any other way.

It's not that I love money for itself. To me it's just a symbol of success, proof to myself and the world that I am in demand. I'm good enough to command big fees. It's a badge of my self-worth. The money signifies that I've made it to the top.

Sometimes that's a problem, though. I'm single, you know. Single but not alone. My life has always been filled with women. I guess I have a way with them. I like women. What I don't like is that because most of the ones I go out with know I do well, they expect me to take them to the most expensive restaurants and to shower them with gifts and flowers. Sometimes I feel that they are making me pay for the privilege of having sex with them. They don't care who I am. They only care about what I can give them.

About a year ago, I decided to escape from it for a couple of weeks by going on a cruise. By myself, of course. On a cruise ship, everything is already covered, so there isn't much you can do to impress a date. In a way, the cruise itself was like one long date, except I picked up my partners after I got there and as I went along.

Our first night at sea, I settled into the ship's routine by having dinner at the table to which I had been assigned. I was seated next to an elegant woman wearing a gown and jewelry that spoke of affluence. She looked to be in her late forties, but I thought she was remarkably well kept. It turns out that was the right expression—well kept. Seated on her other side was an equally elegant gentleman, at least twenty years her senior.

We chatted as tablemates do. During our conversation, I had the sense that she was looking me over the way one of the women I sometimes meet at a singles bar would. Maybe I was flattering myself, but I got the distinct feeling that she was trying to decide what kind of bed partner I would make. Anyway, at some point I mentioned my profession and my specialty. Her partner showed polite interest, but she smiled broadly. When the gentleman left the table for a few minutes, she said that she thought she might have need for my services and asked for my card, intimating that I would receive a call from her when we were back in the city.

A few weeks after the cruise, I was in my office when my secretary told me that Riva Magnussen was on the line. At first, the name meant nothing to me. Then I realized it was the elegant lady I had met on board the ship. I took the call. After we exchanged pleasantries, she said that she wanted to consult me about what she termed a rather delicate matter. I was about to turn her over to my secretary to set up an appointment when she asked if I could drop in on her that evening. I don't usually see clients outside the office, but there was something about the way she said "a rather delicate matter" that made me curious, and the address she gave me was only a couple of blocks away. So I agreed.

When I arrived, she greeted me at the door wearing a long, flowing, and obviously expensive dress. The neckline was rather low, revealing the tops of her ample breasts. Except for her bosom, she was petite, not much more than five-foot-one and small-boned. Her platinum hair hung loose, almost reaching her shoulders. Her beautiful blue eyes captivated me. She was much older than the women I dated, but I found her very attractive.

She led me through an opulently appointed foyer into a spacious and meticulously decorated living room. Indicating a silk upholstered sofa, she mixed me a drink as I sat, and one for herself as well. Although the sofa was long, she took a place close enough so I could smell the subtle fragrance of her perfume. For a moment, we sipped in silence.

She began to describe her living arrangements. She said she was dependent on the generosity of the gentleman I had met on the cruise. He was married but had bought this apartment for her and paid all her expenses. In addition, he provided her with a generous living allowance. I listened attentively, since all that she was telling me seemed relevant to her need for an estate plan. Then the direction of her narrative changed.

She said that her benefactor, as she called him, expected her to be available for his sexual needs once or twice a month and to remain his exclusively. Wistfully, she added that she would not mind this if her needs were attended to as well, but they were not. Oh, she said, all her financial requirements were met quite handsomely. But she was still a vibrant woman. She had sexual needs, too. Much greater than his, apparently.

As she told me this, she moved even closer to me on the sofa. I could feel her thigh pressing against mine. Strangely, I felt a stirring in my groin. Something about this woman, or about the situation, or a combination of the two, was arousing me. Casually, she draped an arm over the back of the couch, just barely touching my shoulders. "You're a very handsome man," she said softly. "I think you could satisfy my needs quite nicely."

I don't exactly know how it happened, but suddenly we were kissing. Her lips were soft and very active. She seemed to be nibbling mine with them as her tongue stole inside my mouth and began dueling with mine. I felt desire building rapidly inside me, much more intense than anything I ever felt with the women I was used to dating.

She took my hand where it lay limp in my lap and guided it to her breast. I was surprised to find that she wore no bra. She was as firm as a young girl, and I could feel the thickness of her nipple against the silky material of her bodice. It was stiff and hard, like my penis was becoming. She began caressing me through my trousers. Involuntarily, I groaned.

As if it had been a signal, she suddenly stood and reached behind her. With a quick movement, she undid the zipper at the back of her dress and removed it. Under it, she wore only the briefest of lacy panties. I could see the blond triangle of her pubic hair through the white lace. Quickly, she stripped them from her and stood naked before me.

I too stood. Without thinking, I shrugged out of my jacket and tossed it onto the couch. I loosened my tie and took it off without bothering to untie it. She was on me then, tearing open my shirt and working at my belt. In seconds, I was nude. Grabbing my shoulders, she pushed me down onto my back on the floor. I felt the carpet, soft and fleecy, against my bare skin.

She was atop me, straddling my hips, rubbing my belly with the wetness of her flowering vulva. She stroked my nipples with her fingertips and rolled them gently one way and then the other. Then, slowly, she took my erect penis in her hand and guided it into her opening as she sank down onto me.

I was entering her a millimeter at a time. It seemed that the penetration would go on forever. Her vagina gobbled a bit of me, and then another, and another. Finally, I felt the hair of her mound tangling with mine. She was wet and hot inside, almost feverish. I felt consumed by her.

With movements that were studied and precise, she began to rotate her hips, seeming to screw me into her deeper and deeper still. I reached up and cupped her breasts in my hands, feeling their weight and heft as she rode me. Her nipples were bright rosy pink and grew longer and thicker as I caressed them. They were crying out for my mouth. Unable to resist, I began sucking and licking them.

A string of meaningless syllables flowed from her lips, in rhythm to the thrusting, rolling movements of her pelvis. She moved with slow erotic grace, elevating the gyrations of intercourse into an exotic form of art. I heard the sounds of our genitals working together, mingling with the music that emanated from her throat. Then, suddenly, she grunted, "Ungh. Yes, right there." It freed me from my own awed silence and allowed me to moan with the pleasure I was feeling.

"Oh, yes," she crooned. "You are so young and strong. You are making me feel so nice. You are fucking me so good." Somehow, the way she introduced the word "fuck" into the elegance of our union aroused me even more. I began to thrash wildly, driving my hips up to bury myself deep inside her and then pressing my buttocks against the carpet to withdraw almost to the tip. Even though she had initiated the action and was on top, I felt that I was in control.

She began to sob. "Oh, I'm so close. Oh, wait for me. Please wait for me."

"I'll wait forever," I whispered. "Come for me. I'll take you there." Placing my hands on the sides of her breasts, so that my fingers were pressed against her ribs, I rolled her over so that now it was I who mounted her. All the while, I kept the rhythm, working my stiff penis in and out of her hot vagina.

"Oh, yes, take me," she sobbed. "Make me your woman."

It took all my strength to keep from coming, but somehow I managed. Every time I felt the semen rising I would clench all the muscles of my groin to hold it back. This made my penis swell and caused her to groan with increased excitement. I continued pumping my thick erection into her, nailing her to the floor with each downstroke and dragging a sigh from her throat with each withdrawing upstroke. Her breath was labored and her voice was hoarse. She seemed to be getting closer and closer but still not arriving.

Then, with a shout, she went tense and stiff all over. "Oh, my God, yes," she wailed. "I don't believe it. Oh, it is happening. Oh, my God ohmyGod ohmyGod." I felt her nails digging into my back and her legs wrapping tightly around my thighs. I ground hard against her, knowing that she was about to come. At last she did.

Her orgasm rose to heights I had never before seen, contracting all the muscles of her body and tightening her vagina so much that I thought it would throttle my penis. She screamed and shouted and moaned and wailed. Finally, when I was sure that she was on the downhill coast, I let my guard down and began to come. I wanted her to know that I had waited for her, so I sighed, "Me too."

We lay on the floor for a few more minutes, our arms and legs entangled. Then she led me to her bathroom, where we showered together. Afterwards, I had to return to the living room for my clothes. As I was dressing, she asked, "How much do you ordinarily bill clients for your time?"

I thought she was just expressing interest in my work, so I answered casually, "Five hundred dollars an hour."

"That sounds fair to me," she said. "You were here an hour and a half." She handed me a bundle of bills.

I was flabbergasted. "What is this?" I stammered.

"I appreciate your service," she said. "I'd like to feel free to call upon you again."

For a moment, in the recesses of my mind, I toyed with the idea of being offended. I was no gigolo. But to tell you the truth, the idea of being paid for sex was very exciting to me. As a matter of fact, the second she handed me the money, I felt my penis getting hard all over again. At that same moment, I realized that while on the floor with her, I had experienced the most powerful orgasm of my life.

"Well," I answered, folding the cash and placing it in my pocket. "You can call upon me anytime." I swear, at that moment I felt it was someone else speaking through my mouth.

"I will," she said. "I know several ladies in the same position as I. May I give them your number?"

Again, someone else seemed to be answering. "Yes," I said. I left it at that.

In the elevator on the way back to the street, I tried to collect my thoughts. I found it impossible. My mind was spinning. Shouldn't I feel debased? I had just taken money for sex. Didn't that make me a male prostitute, a gigolo, one of the lowest creatures on earth?

Yet, I didn't feel debased at all. On the contrary, I felt elated. It was like the feeling I got when I became a partner in the firm. I had been paid—and well paid at that—to have sex with a beautiful, well-kept, and sophisticated woman. I had always thought of myself as a good lover. I know that the women I dated thought so too. But this payment was a tangible symbol of my sexual success. It was proof that I am in demand, good enough to command big fees. It was a badge of my self-worth.

Since then, I have seen Riva a few times, as well as a number of her friends. I still go out with young women and I still spend lavishly on them. I like taking them to bed and I frequently do. But my greatest satisfaction comes when I get a call from a woman who wants to hire me for my sexual services. I like being a man who is good enough to be paid for sex by women who make their livings being paid for sex.

HOUSEWIFE HOOKER

Patti, who just turned thirty-six, is a vivacious woman with a dynamic personality and a smile that makes a person feel comfortable and relaxed. She has a way of looking straight into the eyes of whomever she is talking to, exuding sincerity. Her very black hair is short, thick, and straight, framing her blue-green eyes. Her pale complexion is flawless, but her figure is not. She is maybe five-foot-four and rather chunky. But Patti carries her excess weight with a kind of pride. Once she starts talking, a happy-to-be-alive aura surrounds her. She speaks without any trace of shame about the way she earns extra money.

I'm a housewife hooker and I love every second of it. I love the secrecy of my work. I love the variety of sex I get. Most of all, I love the money I get for doing it. My husband used to think I had a part-time job, but didn't know what it really was. All he ever knew was that it helped him keep up with a very expensive mortgage payment that would really have been over our heads otherwise. Now he thinks I spend my afternoons having tea with the other ladies.

It all started when we moved into a new house in a rather pricy development. I met several other women who had bought in around the same time we did. We didn't have much in common, other than the fact that we all had outgoes that exceeded our incomes. It was clear that our husbands' salaries would never be enough, and that we'd all have to get at least part-time jobs. But we all came from upper-middle-class suburban backgrounds, and none of us had any real experience in the work world.

When we got together for coffee, all we ever talked about was how we were ever going to be able to keep it all together. It didn't take a brain surgeon to come up with the idea of sex for sale. Sex was really the only thing any of us knew about. Obviously, it could be more lucrative than any part-time job we could qualify for. So we talked about it. At first, none of us was really serious. As a plan began to take shape, though, some of us realized that it was something we really could do. A few of the women dropped out when it got beyond the conversational stage, but there were five of us left who decided to give it a try.

Jenny was our leader. She organized our little business and turned out to be quite professional at it, considering the fact that she hadn't worked since a summer job at a fast food place back in her high school days. She said she had a male friend who could supply a few customers to get us started and who would make sure that when any one of us ladies went out on a date, we would be well-protected. We all agreed to give it a shot, with the understanding that each of us could decide to drop out at any time for any reason.

We also agreed that none of us would tell our husbands how we were making the extra money we'd be bringing home. I guess the pressure of finances was so burdensome and the additional income was such a relief that it was easy for them to be fooled by the lies we conjured up. Each of us told her little story, and I guess the men were so glad they weren't drowning in debt that they were ready to accept that we had found a way. I told my husband I was running lingerie parties at other women's homes. He never asked a single question that I couldn't easily come up with an answer for.

I'll never forget the first time I went out on my new occupation. I had told myself that I was giving it just this one chance. If it didn't work out, I would have to find a legitimate means of earning extra money. Jenny's male friend drove me to one of our city's top hotels and accompanied me as far as the lobby. He told me what room to go to and promised he'd be waiting for me in the cocktail lounge. He also said that if he didn't see me in an hour and a half, he'd come up to the room to make sure everything was all right. The last thing he said as I walked away was, "Get the money in advance."

The customer was a businessman who traveled here once a month on business. He had requested a wholesome woman, which is why we all decided I'd be the one. I'm a little on the overweight side.

Well, all right, maybe more than a little. We weren't sure what he meant by "wholesome," but thought maybe it was a code word for "fat." When he saw me, the expression on his face told me that he was satisfied with my appearance.

I had been telling myself that it would be perfectly okay with me if he rejected me. I was nervous as hell about this and told myself that if he didn't like the way I looked, I would take it as a sign that this profession was not for me. When he smiled his approval, I can't tell you what a relief it was. I think that proves that deep down I wanted to go through with it. I was actually looking forward to it. Knowing that Jenny's friend was waiting downstairs for me relieved any fear I had for my physical safety and took some of the pressure off. But I was still nervous as I could be.

Since then, I've learned that many men really like a woman who is overweight. Sometimes they use the expression "BBW," which stands for "big beautiful woman." When talking to clients, Jenny refers to me as "our Zaftig queen." She tells me that "zaftig" is a Yiddish word that means soft and cuddly.

The businessman—let's call him Arthur—sat in the armchair, poured himself a hefty glass of liquor, and asked if I would slowly undress for him. I was feeling very awkward about that but knew that he had a right to call the shots. So I resolved to do my best. When my husband and I were first dating, he too would ask me to strip for him. Whenever I did, it would make both of us very hot. It had been years since we played that way together. So in a way, I even found this stranger's request to be a little exciting.

I stood right in front of him and slowly began to unbutton my white silk blouse. Slipping my arms out, I laid it carefully on a nearby chair. At first, a feeling of embarrassment made me avert my eyes, but I forced myself to look straight into the stranger's face as I undressed for him. I felt a little bit more relaxed when I saw the expression of excitement he was wearing. I reached back to unhook my bra, when Arthur interrupted and asked me to take my skirt off first. So I undid the zipper and let it slide to the floor, leaving me in my half slip. I thrust my fingers inside the waistband, looked over at Arthur for approval, and peeled it off.

I expected to feel embarrassed and ashamed, standing in nothing more than bra and panties in front of a total stranger, but my heart was beating with too much excitement to leave room for any negative feeling at all. I wasn't sure which of us was more turned on by this. I could hear little gurgling tones of sexual hunger coming from his throat, and it heightened my own arousal.

Boldly, I turned to my appreciative audience of one and asked what he wanted me to take off next. When he gestured toward my bra, I obliged. My big tits fell out as I removed it. Even I couldn't believe how hard and huge my nipples had grown. I put my hands under my naked tits and held them up for his inspection. My nipples were fully erect, and little bumps quickly appeared all around, crinkling the dark skin of my areolae. I felt their hardness with my fingers, letting a groan of sexual pleasure escape from my lips.

My hips rotated in little circles, as my fingertips rolled and squeezed my nipples. My own touch felt exhilarating because I could see it was turning him on. I was overwhelmed by the concept of stripping and exhibiting myself to a perfect stranger who would soon be doing as he pleased with my body. The thought of what I had become—a prostitute, a woman who sold her sex for money—was inflaming me. Maybe Arthur's expression of desire had something to do with it. I hadn't seen that look on a man's face in years, and I was hotter and more turned on than I could remember having been.

I licked my fingers and stroked my erect nipples with them till they were all wet and gooey. The more I touched them, the darker they turned and the harder they grew. I was really enjoying myself. The experience was more erotic than any I had ever had with my husband or the handful of men I had known before him. I could feel my panties soaking with the juice of my desire. I had the sensation of liquid flowing down my thighs.

I moved closer to Arthur. Taking my hands from my hot nipples, I very deliberately inched the panties down over my swaying hips and thighs until they reached my knees. Then I let them slide to the floor and stepped out of them. I reached down to touch my pussy and found myself swimming in my own vaginal juice. There was a river of desire rolling through my body, with no end to its insistent tide. Now, with absolutely no embarrassment, I stood close to the stranger in the chair and spread the lips of my vagina, so he could see the hunger I was feeling.

It looked like Arthur's eyes were about to pop out of their sockets. He was moaning softly, his tongue wetting his lips, his eyes riveted to the inside of my hot pussy. The expression on his face and the rasping sound of his breath made me feel sexy and seductive. I kept up a steady gyrating motion with my hips while my fingers pulled back the lips of my vagina for him to see.

It was hard for me to believe that I, a middle-class housewife with three children and a husband, could get so wired up exposing my naked body to a total stranger for money. But there I was—no shame, no guilt. All I felt was sheer horny excitement and a desire to please. My clitoris was emerging from its hiding place, showing its glistening head and begging for attention. Placing my middle finger on the protruding button, I caressed it lightly, all the time aware of the glaring male eyes that seemed to be devouring my nude body.

I turned towards the bed and, without a moment's hesitation, lay down on it on my back. I made sure to position myself so that Arthur had a complete view of my open, bobbing pussy. When I looked up at him, he was standing and stripping off his business suit. I felt a moment of fear, realizing that he would soon be putting his cock in me. Then the fear faded to anticipation. I played with my pussy, pushing my finger in and out of my heated box. I did not dare to touch my clit in fear that I might come too fast. When the women first talked about trying this hooker thing, we had all said that we did not expect to have orgasms. And here I was struggling to hold mine back.

When he removed his pants and underwear, his swollen cock stood out straight in front of him, swaying slightly as he approached the bed. He was completely naked when he sat down beside me, so close I could smell the alcohol on his breath. Leaning towards me, he gently placed his hands on my heaving breasts and started to knead them with his powerful fingers.

It was the first time I had been touched by any man other than my husband since we were married. It was wonderful. My finger continued plucking at my hot pussy while Arthur played with my tits. I was consumed with pleasure. When his fingers zeroed in on my nipples, I began humming with unfeigned desire. "Oh yes," I moaned, almost involuntarily. "That feels wonderful." I looked down to see him skillfully rolling my nipples with his fingers. Wanting to please him, I reached out to touch his hard and throbbing cock.

The skin of his organ was soft and warm to the touch. It was big! Much bigger than my husband's. As I compared them in my mind, I found that the difference excited me. I pulled up and down on it and felt it growing harder and bigger with each tender stroke of my hand. It was amazing that I could derive such pleasure from rubbing a total stranger's penis. The more I stroked him, the bigger it got. Now all I could think about was how it would feel to have his immense tool inside of me.

It was like he read my mind. In an instant, he was on top of me, his knees pushing my legs apart to allow the entry. I could feel the warm flesh of his cockhead parting my pussy lips. My vagina instantly filled with a rush of fluid to accommodate his insertion. Before I could take a deep breath, his mammoth cock entered me. I closed my eyes, wrapped my legs around his, and hugged his back with my waiting arms.

I felt I had never experienced such a huge cock. I groaned at the power of it. When all of his manhood was buried deep inside of me, he slowly started to fuck me. As my body became more relaxed and my vaginal channel softened to accept his plunging cock, he moved with more force. Up and down, hard and fast, he fucked me like I had never been fucked before. I was loving every moment of it.

While his body fucked me hard, his lips and tongue sucked on my heaving nipples. Oh, God, he was good. Just when my pussy had grown accustomed to his large cock, he pulled it out of me. For a second I felt a letdown, a disappointment that the marvelous pleasure he was giving me had stopped. Before I had a chance to understand why, I felt his hands spreading my legs wider. Then his warm breath engulfed my opening.

He licked the outside of my vagina, making my clit crave his attention. Arthur's tongue methodically found its way inside, caressing the inner lips of my pussy and then driving as deep as it could go. My body was thrashing around like a belly dancer's, intoxicated with the fiery torment of sexual hunger. Finally, when I felt the tip of his tongue on my pulsating clitoris, all hell broke loose. My hands wrapped firmly around his head and held it there. He had gone from being my customer to being my lover, and my hands were telling my lover not to stop, commanding him to give me pleasure until I scream for mercy.

I felt his lips circle my clitoris as with soft, slow movements he sucked it lovingly in and out of his mouth. It felt absolutely divine. While my hands held on tightly to the back of his head, my pelvis rocked back and forth meeting every surge. He lapped and licked from my clit to the inner depths of my pussy. I was absolutely wild with excitement.

I never wanted the sensations to stop. I wanted to feel this forever. I couldn't believe sex for sale could ever feel this good. I felt like I was going to explode, and explode I did. As hard as I tried to hold back my climax, there was nothing more I could do. I started to come violently, forgetting that it was my job to pleasure him. With each orgasmic burst, Arthur increased his sucking, until there was not a drop of fluid left for me to squeeze out. I had to push his head away from my body so that I could breathe again.

When Arthur's face moved away from my vagina, he lay down with his back on the mattress. His enormous cock looked even bigger standing straight up in front of him. I reached out and started to caress it. His eyes closed, and his face took on a beatific, almost saintly look. After I stroked it for a time, I bent over and took it into my mouth. Wetting my lips with my own saliva, I gently kissed the head of his cock. When it was completely covered with moisture, I started to suck it as far as I could into my mouth.

His body grew stiff as I sucked deep and hard on his hard-on. Arthur's mouth puckered, and groans of ecstasy escaped his lips. He reached out and grabbed on to my swinging breasts. I let his cock pop out of my mouth and straddled him, inserting him into me with my hand as I lowered my pussy down onto his pelvis. I could feel his pubic hair against me as I began rotating my hips while slamming up and down on his dick. Within moments, a whirlwind of sperm shot into my pussy. As he came, his body moved wildly, desperately keeping pace with his orgasm.

When he was all spent, his large hands let go of my breasts and a deep sigh of relief issued from his mouth. That was when I remembered the final instructions I had received: "Get the money first." I realized that if Arthur decided not to pay me, there would be no way to repossess his orgasm. Then I mentally shrugged, thinking that in a way, he had paid by giving me the hottest time I could ever remember.

Of course, my worry had been for nothing. After we took a while to catch our breath, Arthur got up and started to dress, I knew it was my cue to do the same. As he pulled up his pants, he thanked me profusely for what he called a glorious experience. He asked if I would be interested in seeing him again. I said I'd be glad to see him again, and I meant it. I was trying to think of how to bring up the money, when I saw him reach into his pocket. The agreed price was three hundred dollars, but he gave me five hundred. For me, that was the real climax. Would you believe it if I told you that I felt myself getting excited all over again?

The money said something to me. It said that I was desirable. The extra two hundred said I was even more desirable than he had expected. It made me feel more like a woman than any experience I ever had. It's a feeling I get whenever I take money from a sex customer.

Oh, yes, I've had many since Arthur. I'm still screwing strangers for a price, but the funny thing is we don't really need the money anymore. Not for the usual reasons, anyway. After I had been hooking for about three months, my grandfather died and left me a nice life insurance policy. With that inheritance, the mortgage payments stopped being a problem.

I still like the money, though. Not for what it buys, but for what it makes me feel when I'm receiving it. Always in advance, now, I might add. It proves that I have something valuable to offer. It proves I'm sexy. It proves I'm a woman.

I've given up telling my husband about lingerie parties that I never really conducted anyway. I haven't told Jenny or the others about the inheritance, and I'm still hooking. I only take dates in the afternoon, so I don't have to give my husband any explanation whatsoever. I spend the money on myself, mainly for expensive undergarments to further please my customers. What I don't spend, I put in a bank account that my husband knows nothing about. Who knows? We might need it someday. But even if we never do, I intend to keep fucking for money as long as there are men willing to pay me.

4

SEX-DOT-COM

JUST ABOUT EVERY LIST OF THE MOST INFLUENTIAL people of the second millennium includes the name of Johannes Gutenberg. In the 1450s, he changed the course of history by making 180 copies of the bible on his new printing press. According to Danish researcher Berl Kutchinsky, the first printed pornography appeared in the 1650s, with the publication of three works, *La Puttana Errante* ("The Wayward Prostitute"), *L'Ecole des Filles* ("The Girls' School"), and *Satya* ("The Truth"). That was two hundred years after Gutenberg's invention.

At the end of the 1960s, the history of communication was changed again forever when Arpanet was born. It soon became what we now know as the Internet. It took only a few years for pornography to find its way onto the Internet. Now it is available there in virtually all the important languages of our time.

Some people use the Internet for business. Some use it to further their education. Some use it for recreation. To the people who tell their stories in this chapter, the Internet is a source of sexual satisfaction.

For the woman calling herself "BBW_QT," the Internet provides her only sexual interaction with other people. Although she is inhibited about sexual contact in the real world, cybersex fulfills her needs. The man who uses the Internet handle "Hard14U" describes himself as being in the singles scene, where sex is first on everyone's mind but the last thing anyone talks about. He thinks that if he ever told one of the women he meets what he's really interested in doing, he'd soon be sitting alone. So, like BBW_QT, he has made the Internet the focal point of his erotic lifestyle.

VIDEO CONFERENCE

We never met Hard14U in person. Our only communication was by e-mail. He describes himself as six-foot-two, 195 pounds, twenty-seven years old, very fit, and a firefighter. His description is peppered, however, with the abbreviations "LOL," which stands for "laughing out loud," and "LMAO," which stands for "laughing my ass off." These are Internet conventions used to let the reader of a communication know that the statements made in it are not to be taken seriously. For all we know, Hard14U may be a short, skinny, unemployed woman of seventy-two.

The nice thing about the Internet is that nobody gets to know any more about you than you want them to know. That's what makes it so easy for me to find play partners. Everyone feels secure. They shed their inhibitions the moment they enter the chatrooms.

I've always liked jerking off in company. When I was thirteen, I used to get together with a bunch of my friends for what we called "circle jerks." We'd all put up a quarter and sit around masturbating. The first one to come would win the money. The pot never amounted to more than maybe a dollar or a dollar and a half. I guess we all realized that the money was only an excuse. We were doing it mainly for the thrill of being watched and watching each other.

As far as I know, all the boys in that crowd grew up to be straight.

I'm sure we would have preferred playing the game with girls, but we couldn't find any who were interested. By the time I was in high school, though, that changed.

My school was big on sex education. We were so inundated with information about AIDS and other sexually transmitted diseases that most of us were terrified of having sex with anyone. You know how it is at that age. Sex is all a high school kid can think of, boys and girls alike. I can't say how the other kids handled it, but I managed to find several girls who, like me, used self-stimulation as an outlet and were only too glad to do it in groups. At least it was safe.

We'd have impromptu parties on afternoons when somebody had a house to themself. Five or six of us would gather to watch each other masturbate. Usually, we'd sit around in somebody's living room with all the shades closed. The guys would drop their pants and shorts around their ankles, and the girls would lift their skirts or pull down their pants and lower their panties. Then we'd use hands and fingers on ourselves, watching each other stroke and diddle until everyone came.

As we got older, people tended to drop out. I guess they felt ashamed or embarrassed. As time went on, we all started dating and getting involved in real sex with girlfriends and boyfriends. Eventually, the group masturbation thing was phased out altogether. I really missed it, though. In my senior year of high school, I was fucking two different girls and loving it, but it didn't give me quite the same thrill as those early circle jerk sessions.

I did manage to get into one group masturbation experience when I was in college. I was with a casual girlfriend and another couple at a Friday-night football game. We were passing a flask and all had more to drink than we should have. Winona, the girl I was with, was the least drunk, so she drove us back to the dorm from the game. We still had some booze left, so we decided to finish it in the room that Winona shared with Terry, the other girl we were with.

Terry's date, Vaughn, was probably the drunkest of us. As soon as we got into the room, he fell onto the bed and said, "How about an orgy?" He was laughing hysterically when he said it, so no one really took him seriously. I noticed Terry whispering something in Winona's ear.

"Hey," I said. "What's that all about? No secrets here."

Winona giggled. "I don't think it's any secret," she said. "Terry told me she's horny. I'll bet we all are."

Vaughn came out of his drunken laughter to shout that he was too. I added my agreement to the consensus. Winona giggled again. "Too bad there's nothing we can do about it," she said. "Unless Terry and Vaughn have someplace else to go."

I probably wouldn't have said anything if I hadn't been drunk, but I began telling them about the group masturbation games I had played with my male friends when I was a kid, and then in mixed company when I was in high school. If they hadn't been as drunk as I was, they probably would have made fun of me and just laughed the whole thing off. Instead, Vaughn stood up on wobbly legs and undid his belt buckle.

He unzipped his fly and dropped his pants around his ankles before sitting down again. He slurred, "Hey, I'm game." He was not wearing underwear and his cock stood up straight from his lap. He started stroking it immediately.

I could see both girls looking at him and getting horny expressions. Winona turned to me. "Well?" she questioned. "This was your idea. What about it?" Not to be outdone, I dropped my pants and shorts, too. I wasn't fully erect, but there was enough for me to grab and hold in my hand.

Winona and Terry looked at each other and sort of shrugged. Terry was wearing a one-piece jumpsuit. She unzipped it down the front and stepped out of it. Under it were a lacy red bra and teeny-weeny red thong panties. Taking a cue from her roommate, Winona peeled off her jeans and sweater, standing in white cotton panties and a white bra. She pirouetted in place and then sat on a straight-back study chair. Terry sat beside her in a similar chair. Both girls pulled their panties off. Terry unsnapped and removed her bra as well.

The sight of the two girls first in their underwear and now just about naked made me hard, and I started stroking in earnest. My eyes moved from Terry's pointy little tits to Winona's hairy pussy to Terry's shaved crotch and back to Terry's tits. I was in heaven. As the two girls began stroking themselves, my cock started to tingle.

Terry began by playing with her tight pink nipples. She pulled them gently, until they looked like they were a good inch and a half long. Then she moved her hands in little circles around them, making the pink disks tighten up and get pebbly. She kept that up with one hand while the other began rubbing her snatch.

Winona kept her bra on, but cupped her bigger, rounder breasts through it. I could see the nubs of her erect nipples straining at the material. I had slept with her a couple of times and had held those nipples in my hands, but seeing her play with them in this group setting was more exciting than anything I had done with her up to then. When the nipples were as hard as they were going to get, she used one hand to hold the lips of her pussy apart while the fingers of her other hand took turns plunging inside it. I could see that she had elevated masturbation to an art. With practiced gestures, she carried moisture from her open snatch to her clit and rubbed little figure-eights around it.

Without even thinking about it, I was jerking my cock mercilessly, pulling it hard up and down. Occasionally, I glanced over at Vaughn. He was so involved in playing with his prick that he seemed to have forgotten about the females. He was looking down at his own crotch, as though the sight of it turned him on. He held his hard-on in both hands, sort of twisting them in different directions while moving them up and down.

It was an interesting technique, so I began trying it myself. The difference was that I was very much aware of the women. I watched them intently as I masturbated. The best part was knowing that they were watching me as I was watching them.

For each of us, the sight of the others and the knowledge that we were on display were like aphrodisiacs. If any of us felt any inhibitions when this began, they were certainly gone now. I tried moving my hands in a way that would keep them from covering my cock so I could be sure the girls would see. I'm certain they were doing something similar.

Winona was leaning way back in the chair, her legs splayed wide. Her bush was so full and thick that hair was showing all around her masturbating hand. To increase the eroticism of her exhibition, she was spreading her pussy lips so that I could see the beefy color inside.

Terry, sitting right next to her, had a more delicate-looking pussy. The fact that it was shaved made the labia and clitoral hood stand out in bold relief. She moved her fingers gracefully, keeping only the very tips in contact with her sensitive tissues. I could see moisture oozing from her crack as she got more and more excited.

I have relived that evening many times. I remember the tremendous stimulation I received from what I was seeing and from the knowledge that they were seeing me. It was even arousing to look at Vaughn's hands sliding up and down on his swollen cock. Watching the girls look from my cock to his and back again while they rubbed their sweet pussies for him and me to see was just about the most erotic experience I've ever had.

It wasn't long before I felt the cum building. At first, I was embarrassed to be getting off so fast. Then I realized that all four of us were hovering on that tormenting brink of orgasm. So I decided to start the ball rolling. "Mmmmmm," I groaned. "Watch me. I'm going to come."

Both women stared at my cock. Even Vaughn came out of his drunken reverie to look in my direction. Let me tell you, it was a thrill to have all three of them watching me as the first spurt of hot gizz shot from the end of my prick. I really started to ham it up. "Oooh, yeah," I wailed. "Oh, God, yes. Ooh, my God, I'm coming so good."

I guess I set the pace, because all of them started to come right around the same time. Everyone seemed to be trying to outdo each other with songs of climax. The air was filled with heated cries of passion as the four of us exhibited our sexuality to one another. When we were finished, we all laughed. The laughter must have continued for a good five minutes.

It would have been so nice to repeat the performance, but we never did. I saw Winona for a while after that, but every time I tried to bring up that night, she would get flustered and change the subject. Eventually, I went on to other women. Presumably, she went on to other men.

That was quite a while ago, of course. Now I'm in the singles scene, dating and hoping, dating and hoping. It's a strange sort of subculture, this world of young single people looking for partners, looking for mates. We all walk on eggshells. Sex is what we want more than anything, yet we're not supposed to admit that. Instead, we talk to each other about our work, about skiing, about books we've read and movies we've seen, about everything except what really matters. I'm sure if I ever told a woman I've met in a cocktail lounge or at a party that I'd like to watch her masturbate while she watches me, I'd be sitting alone within seconds.

That's where the Internet comes in. I go to a video conferencing chatroom regularly. That's a place on the Internet where people can talk and see each other at the same time. All you need is a webcam. They cost maybe seventy-five bucks, and you don't have to be any kind of computer genius to hook one up. It's plug and play, all the way. "Plug and play" is a programming system that makes it possible for idiots like me to add new gizmos to their computers without knowing anything at all. Just plug it in and the computer does the rest.

Anyway, I turn on the cam and go the chatroom. There, they have a list of all the people who are online at the moment, with a little description of what each is looking for. Nobody uses their right name. My handle is "Hard14U." Get it? That's "Hard One for You." My description says I'm looking for masturbation partners. On almost any day, I can find a guy or two and a woman or two who have the same interests as I. I get all of them on my screen, and they get me and each other on their screens. Most people aim the cams at their genitals, or the women at their tits, so that you can't see their faces. Then we play.

By play, I mean we talk to each other while playing with ourselves and watching the others do the same. The Internet is international, you know. I might see a guy from Russia stroking his twelve-inch dick while I watch a fat black woman from Jamaica fiddling with her tits, and a skinny white blonde in Ireland sticking a dildo in her pussy. Some people in the chatroom are choosy, but I'm not. I'll play with just about anybody. I don't care about age, color, shape, nationality, or even gender. As long as they're watching me and I'm watching them, I'm excited and will be satisfied.

In the real world, I play the dating game and have conventional sex with conventional people. Grown-ups, if you know what I mean. In cyberspace, I get to do what I really like with people I know only by their handles and who know me only by my handle. All I ever show them is my cock and my balls, so I can tell them anything I want about the way I look, my age, my occupation. I tell them whatever I feel like saying at the time. I know they're all doing the same. What difference does it make? Cocks and pussies—that's what it's really about.

I do it almost every day, so I think you can call it an erotic lifestyle, even if it's only cyber erotica. It's just about the greatest thing that could have happened for a guy like me. Probably, I'll find Ms. Right and get married someday. Maybe when that happens I'll be able to tell her whet I really like. My hope is that she'll come into the chatroom with me and we can play together. In the meantime, I'm quite satisfied with what I'm doing.

POSTING PIX

"BBW_QT" is the Internet handle of a woman who contacted us by e-mail. She describes herself as five feet four inches and 285 pounds of big, beautiful woman. We never met her in person, but she sent us pho-

tographs of herself in the nude. From them, her description appears to be accurate. We can add that she has huge breasts, wide hips, and seems to be in her early to mid-thirties. In one of the pictures, she has her back to the camera and is bending over to show her large, round, smooth-skinned bottom.

The Internet saved my self-respect. To look at me now, you wouldn't believe it, but I used to be slim, trim, and fit. I didn't even have to work at it. I wasn't into sweets and didn't eat much in general. Two or three times a year, I'd go on a binge. When that happened, I'd eat everything in sight. Once, I ate three gallons of ice cream in an afternoon, all by myself.

The last one of those binges stretched from three days to three weeks. Then three months. Then three years. Finally, it became permanent. You might say I'm still on it. In a very short time, I gained more than 150 pounds.

The weight gain played havoc with my sex life. In fact, I no longer had one. I'm not sure if the guy I was seeing at the time was turned off by the fat. I just sort of assumed he was and stopped going out with him. I kept myself out of the dating market because I thought that "fat" meant "ugly." I always believed I'd lose the weight and be pretty again. It never happened.

The sexual frustration was driving me nuts. Somehow, though, it wasn't enough to motivate me to lose the excess pounds. I mean, let's face it, 150 pounds is a lot of excess to lose. I even got to thinking in terms of kilograms. Sixty-eight kilos didn't seem nearly as bad. But the mirror doesn't lie. I was convinced no one would want me in this shape.

I tried to be content with self-fulfillment. My tits were bigger than ever, and I played with them a lot. It felt very good when I cupped them in my hands, because I think every woman wants to have mammoth titties. If only the mammoth belly and thighs didn't have to go with them.

I would rub my pussy a lot, too, even though the fact that I couldn't see it depressed me. Sometimes, I'd lay on my back and hold my legs in the air and use a mirror to look at my pussy. It was the only part of me that didn't get any bigger. Looking at it would actually get me turned on.

I'd put my fingers in it and rub my clit until I came over and over again. Still, I didn't feel fulfilled. I mean, masturbation is all right. I know that for many women it's the only way to have orgasms. I used to have orgasms with men, but I always liked masturbating, even in my slim days.

There is nothing like having a partner, though. Someone to tell you how great you look. Someone to excite you by getting excited with you. You know what I mean? I was beginning to think I'd never enjoy that kind of sexual pleasure again. Then I found out about the BBW website.

"BBW" is Internet slang for "big beautiful woman." Someone told me that this website was specifically devoted to women built like I am. I looked it up, thinking it might be a place to get information about weight loss, which is what I thought was uppermost in the mind of every big woman. Notice I say "big woman" because I just couldn't accept that the second "B" stood for "beautiful." I could not see how "big" and "beautiful" could possibly go together.

When I went to the website, I discovered that not everyone saw it that way. What a surprise. There are actually men who prefer fat women. Even better, there are fat women who like being fat. They think it's sexy. They know they are more attractive to certain men than skinny women are. It was a real eye-opener.

The women would post pictures—"pix," they call them in Internet slang—of themselves naked. They weren't trying to hide their fat. They were flaunting it. They'd squeeze their tits in their hands until the boob flesh overflowed in all directions. They'd photograph themselves lying back with their thick legs apart to show their naked pussies. They'd bend over and show their giant butts. They'd revel in their own rotund bellies and big asses.

They'd give themselves handles like "BigFatSlut" or "Chubby-Gal4U." I remember one in particular who called herself "AssAMileWide." Some would just post the pix and solicit comments. Others would list their e-mail addresses and ask for mail from the men who saw them. A few would ask the men to print out their pictures, masturbate on them, and send the BBW a shot of the BBW's picture with the man's cum on it. I couldn't believe what I was seeing and reading.

Men would post comments in which they talked about how turned on the big women made them. Some would say that they'd give anything to do this or that to the woman in the pic. They would describe their fantasy sex acts in detail. How they'd put their tongue in the woman's ass, or suck her pussy until she had a dozen orgasms, or titty-fuck her until they covered her nipples with cum. They weren't turned on *in spite of* the fact that the women were fat, but *because* of it.

At first, I had trouble believing what I saw and read there. Nothing in my experience prepared me for this connection between being fat and being sexy. I had always been taught, or told, or demonstrated in some way, that fat was the opposite of sexy. I truly believed that there was no place in the erotic world for overweight women. It took a while for me to get adjusted to the idea that this might not be so.

I went back to the website every day. Sometimes I would spend hours there, looking at the posted pix and reading the men's comments. I began to play with the idea of posting some pix of myself. I had never read a single ugly word in the men's comments, so I wasn't too afraid of rejection. Of course, I wouldn't have to use my real name or show my face, so even if someone wanted to reject me, they'd never know who I was. I'd just be another naked fat body.

First I had to get a digicam—that's a digital camera—so I could download pix directly to the computer and upload them to the website. The one I originally bought cost just a little more than a hundred dollars. I have a better one now. I also got a tripod, so I could set it up and take pictures of myself, and a remote-control cable that allowed me to snap it from a distance.

My first photo session was pretty clumsy. None of the pix was what I had hoped for. Somehow, I had something artistic in mind. What I got were sex pix. No art at all. Just shots of my bare titties and my open pussy. I wasn't sure I wanted to post anything like that, but finally, I went ahead and did it.

I was shocked. Men started posting comments immediately. So many of them, it was incredible. They said they found me hot. They found me sexy. They told me I was hot pron—that's Internet slang for "pornographic." One even called me an erotic goddess. They said they wanted to see more of me. They had suggestions for how I should pose in the next set.

Believe me, they weren't interested in art. They wanted to see me holding my pussy open. They wanted to see my asshole. They wanted to see me sucking my own nipples. One of them said he wanted to see me in sheer pantyhose. I hadn't worn pantyhose since I got fat. His response made me feel so good, I went out and bought a pair of queen-size that same day.

Later that night, I shot some more pix, in and out of the pantyhose. I was positively shameless. I did hold my pussy open for the men to see. I did suck my own nipples, something I was only able to do after I gained weight and my tits got so big. I boldly showed my asshole. I posted the pix without thinking twice. It was only after I saw them at the website that I began to feel a sense of embarrassment.

That faded, though, when I read the comments men posted to the second set. I sat in front of my computer looking at my own pix and reading what people were saying about them, and I masturbated over and over again. It felt better than masturbation ever had before. I was hooked.

When I posted a third set, I listed my e-mail address and asked men to send me pix of their cocks. Within hours, my e-mail inbox was flooded with responses. They were filled with filthy descriptions about how the guys who were writing would give me pleasure. They described the way they'd nibble my clit, or tongue-fuck my ass, or suck my tits. They attached pix of their own cocks. In many of them, cum was dribbling from the tips. I masturbated as I read and looked, coming repeatedly.

Since then, I've been posting pictures on a regular basis. I visit the website at least twice a week, uploading pix of myself almost every time. My mailbox is always filled with e-mails from men who have seen my pix and want to get in touch with me. Some offer to have phone sex with me or to come and see me, but I haven't done anything like that. I'm perfectly content to show myself to the Internet world and to masturbate while reading the responses I get.

That's the extent of my sex life at the moment, but it's really pretty good. One day I'll take one of my admirers up on his offer to come see me. Now that I know that "fat" is not the same as "undesirable," I'm sure I'll find my soul mate and live happily ever after. I won't give up my erotic lifestyle, though. I owe it a lot.

5

I DO, YOU DO, WE ALL DO

"POLYAMORY" IS A WORD THAT HAS ENTERED OUR vocabulary so recently that it still is not found in most dictionaries. Although the term comes from the roots *"poly,"* meaning "more than one," and *"amor,"* meaning "love," one of the people who tells her story in this chapter says that for her love has very little to do with it. Until its meaning is stabilized by lexicographers, the name probably will be given loosely to any relatively permanent domestic bond between more than two partners.

Theoretically, sex need not be part of a polyamorous relationship. Most of the time it is, however. The combinations of three or more lovers are not orgies or instances of group sex, but families of a somewhat unconventional sort.

Evelyn describes a ceremony that was performed to unite her and her two husbands, with all three of them saying "I do" while connected by their genitalia. She recognizes that the ritual had no legal significance, but she introduces the men as her husbands and they both regard her as their wife. She doubts that the three-way honeymoon will ever end.

Job is more matter-of-fact about his connection to Neda and Wendy, both of whom he considers his wives. He does not describe their relationship as polyamorous. In all likelihood he has never heard the word. He and his wives sleep together in one bed, where one frequently watches him having sex with the other. He adamantly insists that he would never make love to both his mates at the same time, referring to such behavior as sick and perverted. Unlike Evelyn, who believes that her erotic lifestyle is a little on the weird side, Job seems to regard his as something perfectly natural.

TWO HUSBANDS

Evelyn is thirty-nine years old and keeps herself looking youthful. She's slim and very active. When we asked if she works out, she sort of giggled and said that we could call it working out, but it really was just part of her erotic lifestyle. She is five feet nine inches tall, with black hair that comes halfway down her back. Her light blue eyes stand out against her white skin and she has a pair of dimples that flatter her thick puckered lips. In answer to a question about whether the pucker is surgically augmented, she just smiles. She works for a large advertising agency, but is more interested in talking about her personal life than about her work.

I always remember knowing myself as a highly stimulated sexual human being. That sex hunger is what got me into my present lifestyle. The literature calls it "polyamory," which literally means "loving more than one." I'll admit something to you, even though I don't think I'd say it to my husbands. We all recognize that in the beginning, love had nothing to do with it, but I'm not sure there is really any true love involved now, either.

Beginning when I was twelve years old, all I could think of was sex. I found it hard to concentrate on my studies in school because everything had some sexual meaning for me. Of course, at that age, all pubescent girls have raging hormones and do a lot of what I call vaginal thinking. Heaven knows their brains are definitely not involved. I was quite different from my girlfriends though. They were all sexually curious. Some of them let boys feel their budding little tits occasionally, or even grope their burning twats. But none of them was having sexual intercourse, like I was.

I didn't have a boyfriend. I just fucked all my big brother's friends. Most of them were seventeen or so, and they were so glad to find a willing female that they didn't care about the fact that I was little more than a child. I was just barely developing a bush when I got started.

By the time I was sixteen, I was pregnant. That was almost a quarter century ago. Things were very different then. I thought my parents would kill me when they found out. His too. The only thing for us to do was get married. Love had nothing to do with it that first time, either. We had no choice. The irony is that I had a miscarriage four months into my pregnancy. So we got married for nothing.

At first, it was great to have sex without guilt, but that didn't last very long. I got bored with him and with the sex. In no time, I had a handful of boyfriends on the side. Not long after it began, we had the marriage dissolved. I was not quite nineteen, single again, and masturbating three or four times a day.

I dated every Tom, Dick, and Harry in sight, but no male was ever able to satisfy my insatiable lust. I went from one to another but never felt fulfilled. Either the sex became monotonous, or there just wasn't enough of it. Just when I would be warming up, my partner would be running down. I made a lot of guys angry, because no matter how seriously I committed to one man, I'd always end up cheating. I couldn't help it. I always needed more than one could give me.

I realized I'd never be able to get married again, for that reason. Any marriage I got into would be doomed from the start. So I tried to satisfy my needs by going out with lots of different men. It was a way of getting all the sex I needed. But it didn't satisfy those other needs. I mean the ones that are planted deep in the DNA. The need to settle down, have a home, have a steady partner. I don't just mean someone to fuck. I mean someone to sleep with and wake up with. To have morning coffee with. Someone to have history with.

When I first met Joe, I just saw him as a big, strong, good-looking man, with a body like Atlas. He had a dynamic personality as well. Maybe if I had been looking for a permanent partner, he would have been a candidate, but like I said, I wasn't. Sex between Joe and me was good. As could be expected, though, it just wasn't enough. For one thing, he couldn't keep up with me. No man could. For another, the same cock gets tiresome after a while, when it's the only one you get to see, touch, taste, and have inside you.

Joe was always hinting about getting serious with me. By then, I had learned enough to be honest about my sexuality. So I explained that as much as I liked him, he just wouldn't be enough to satisfy me. Rather than making promises I couldn't keep, I preferred having it stay casual. But Joe surprised me by introducing me to a new way of looking at life and at sex. He changed my whole perspective.

It all started one night when we had planned to get together for an evening of sex at his apartment. Joe called me just as I was getting ready to leave and said that his brother was visiting with him. I was disappointed, because I had been looking forward to the sex. When I said that, Joe said that was okay. I should come over and he was sure we'd find a way.

When I got there, he introduced me to his brother, Peter. They looked nothing alike, although they were only a year apart in age. Joe is a giant of a man, while Peter is a bit of a shrimp. I just made up my mind that it was going to be a night without sex. We drank a little wine and talked for a while, but I was getting antsy. I really had been looking forward to fucking with Joe, and now the best I'd be able to do would be to masturbate when I got home.

I was thinking about making up some excuse and leaving to see if I could find another date for the evening, when Joe said, "You know, Evelyn, I was telling Peter how good you are in the bedroom, and he's dying to see for himself." I was a little startled. In spite of all my promiscuity, I was not crazy about the idea of being passed from brother to brother, like a wine bottle in a brown paper bag. I was about to get angry, when Joe startled me again, by saying, "I think between us, Peter and I can give you a better time than I ever could alone."

I realized then that he was talking about a threesome. That was something I had never tried before. It just hadn't ever come up. The thought of it was rather exciting. Two men at once would have to be at least twice as good as one man at a time. I decided to give it a try. "Why not?" I said, trying to sound more casual than I actually felt. "Let's see what you brothers can do."

We walked straight into the bedroom, where Peter was the first to take off all his clothes. I watched intently, never taking my eyes off of his rock-hard, swollen penis. He was a little guy, but he had a huge cock. It stood straight out in front of him, twitching a little with anticipation.

Joe then disrobed until he, too, was completely naked. Of course, I had seen Joe's cock before that night, so there was nothing there to surprise me. But being able to look from one cock to the other was exciting. The knowledge that I'd be having both these brothers at once and would be feeling both their cocks at the same time made it even hotter.

I saw the two of them looking over at me and realized that was my cue to join them. I quickly shrugged out of my red dress and wasted no time removing my bra and panties. Now I stood before them as naked as they were, curious to see where this was going to go.

My breasts were firm and my nipples ached with excitement. Joe and Peter stood beside me. There was a full-length mirror on the wall, and I watched the three of us in it. Peter hadn't said much when we were all sitting and making conversation. I thought he was shy. But with his clothes off, he was a different man completely. He was aggressive and forward.

Without a second's hesitation, he walked behind me and brushed his hard-on against the cheeks of my naked ass. I lifted my arms so he could reach around me to cup my ample breasts with both of his hands. He fondled them expertly, kneading and running his fingers over the smoothness of my silky skin.

Joe sat on the edge of the bed in front of me, his knees between my long tapering legs. I had them spread apart slightly, and his face came right up to my purring twat. His fingers toyed with my pubic hair until the lips of my pussy started to part. I watched all this in the mirror and couldn't believe the current of excitement that was beginning to build inside me. Joe's big strong fingers pulled lightly at my silken pussy hairs until they worked their way toward my parted lips. Gently easing them open, he moved his head to one side, so I could look straight into the mirror and see the heated pink flesh staring right back at me. Then he slipped his middle finger inside and began working it in and out.

Peter's fingers were rolling the tips of my nipples while his hands cupped the mounds of my breasts. Gasping garbles were cooing from my mouth. Never before had I experienced two men pleasing me at the same time. I couldn't believe the pleasure it was giving me. As Joe stroked and petted my pussy, I felt the tip of Peter's cock just slightly parting the cheeks of my ass. Removing one of his hands from my breast, he used it to place his penis right up against my tight rear opening. He returned to my nipple, but I could feel the heat from the head of his cock warming my anus. I pressed my body back and he pressed his forward until I could feel him starting to enter the tight little opening.

Every erogenous zone was being touched—my breasts, my nipples, my pussy, my anus. Joe's finger was fucking me steadily now, and my vagina was swallowing it up and coating it with an abundance of thick, heavy juice. My clitoris was absolutely huge and jutted out, showing its purple head. I could see its protrusion in the mirror as it tingled and begged to be touched. I felt Joe's finger stroke it gently, and I closed my eyes to soak in all the glorious sensations that four hands were providing.

The physical contact felt good to my skin and body. But the most erogenous zone of all, my mind, was being stimulated even further by the thought of what was going on. Two men were sharing me. Brothers. They were working together to bring me pleasure. There were four hands, two cocks, two scrotums filled with hot balls. Everything was doubled. Somehow, it seemed that because they were brothers, they had a special understanding between them that would bring them together in perfect harmony to tantalize and satisfy me.

My body rocked back and forth and my hips swayed with the rhythms of sex. The movement allowed the cheeks of my ass to part and made Peter's cock work its way deeper inside me. My anus was being stretched to the max, but, strangely, I wanted more. It wasn't the kind of desire that comes with dissatisfaction, but the kind that was increased by the ecstasy I was experiencing for the first time.

Joe's face was moving in closer to my pussy. He puffed his hot breath onto it. My clit grew larger with each blast of warm air. At last, I felt the moist tip of his tongue touch it lightly. My knees started to buckle. You just can't imagine the pleasures, the sensations, the bliss I was feeling. Words cannot do it justice. All I know is that it was driving me wild. Joe's tongue nibbled and sucked on my clit, while his hands glided gently up and down the insides of my thighs.

Peter's body rocked back and forth as he fucked my ass, each driving thrust of his pelvis forcing his cock a little deeper into the circle of my anus. His hands and fingers never stopped massaging my breasts and nipples. The three of us were having the time of our lives.

Joe's tongue went from my clit to the inside of my pussy and back again. Suddenly, he rose to his feet, his cock as hard as a rock. He took it in both his hands and started to rub it. I watched in the mirror at first, and then looked directly at him, hungrily watching him jerk his cock up and down like he always did just before putting it inside me. I realized I was about to be made into a sandwich, with Peter's cock in my ass and Joe's in my pussy.

He masturbated for just a few seconds and moved in closer. First he pressed it flat and hard against the soft lips of my pussy, not trying to get it in, but just wetting the length of his hard-on with the juices of my excitement. Reaching around behind me, he took hold of my ass cheeks and pulled them apart to allow his brother's swollen cock to penetrate my anus even more deeply. Then, pulling me towards him, he pressed the tip of his hard-on against the opening of my slit and slipped it inside.

Onward he drove, until my pubic hair was tangling with his. In the mirror, I watched his ass move as he fucked one opening and his brother fucked the other. Peter's hands squeezed gently at my tits, enhancing the pleasure of the double penetration. The smaller brother's big cock had moved all the way in, buried to the hilt in the clinging heat of my anal passage.

I was getting it from both ends. While Joe moved in one direction, Peter moved in another. I was so excited that it felt like every part of my body was climaxing without stop. My breasts were having an orgasm. My nipples felt like they were spitting gism. My clit was shooting blasts of climactic sensations. My head whirled with torrential excitement.

All three of us were moving in unison. The sounds I heard escaping from all of our mouths were like none I had ever heard before. We no longer were part of the earth, but drifting somewhere else in an outer atmosphere. It was absolutely wild and terrific. Peter was the first to come. I felt his body stiffen a bit and then I felt his hands on my breasts start to spasm. I heard a groaning sound from his lips and felt his cock start to spurt. My ass filled to overflowing with his semen. I felt it dripping down the backs of my thighs.

His climax aroused me so that I started to join him in the explosion. My pussy was getting even hotter and wetter. All I could do was scream as my orgasm began. It took over my entire being. The earth fell away. Joe's cock moved in and out steadily, never missing a beat, until he too joined in. A gush of warm fluid filled my pussy while he kept pumping hard and furiously.

When our orgasms subsided and all three of us had returned to this planet, Joe and Peter moved me over onto the bed and the three of us collapsed onto the king-size mattress. Just as I was catching my breath, the two of them started to lick and suck my pussy. For the first time in my life, I felt I needed recovery time. I begged them to wait, but they paid no attention to my demands. At first, the sensations felt like more than I could stand, but seconds into it, I started feeling all hot again.

The crazy three-way sex went on into the wee hours of the morning, when all of us fell into a deep exhausted sleep. I was only vaguely aware when, an hour or so later, Joe rolled me onto my back, climbed on top of me, and fucked me until he came. Thirty minutes after that, I was adrift in a sea of unconsciousness when Peter spooned against me, slipped his cock into my pussy from behind and bucked roughly until both of us came.

The following day was more of the same. Joe went out for a while to buy some groceries and beer, and while he was gone Peter ate me until I came three times. When Joe returned, Peter went into the kitchen to put the groceries away while Joe bent me over the arm of a chair and fucked me until I came again. Then Peter came back into the room, and the two of them made love to me again. This time, Joe lay on his back and I lay with my back against his chest while Peter held my pussy open and inserted his brother's cock. Then, while Joe fucked me, Peter sucked my clit and played with my tits until I had one crashing orgasm after another.

I returned to Joe's house every night for two weeks, submitting myself to every sexual whim either of them or I could think of. Sometimes the three of us got it on together. Sometimes one of them would leave for some reason and I'd fuck the other. Sometimes one would just watch while I did the other or the other did me. During that whole time, I never even thought about another man. Why would I? For the first time in my life, I was being totally satisfied.

It was just too good to be true. I was afraid it was going to end. One night, when I arrived at Joe's place, the two men were wearing serious expressions. I was sure they were about to break the news that Peter was leaving, or that they had grown tired of me, or were no longer able to keep up the pace. I was surprised when, instead, in rehearsed unison, they said, "Evelyn, we make a great team. Will you marry us?"

Of course I thought that they were kidding. Marry them both? They must have just been saying that to show that they really liked me. So I laughed. Joe got even more serious, saying, "No, we mean it. We can be good husbands to you. We think we've shown you that you'll never be bored sexually if you hook up with us. If you ever do get bored, we promise to understand and let you go."

I couldn't believe what I was hearing. They actually meant it. I just laughed again and said, "Well, let's see how many times you can make me come tonight. Then, if you can find a minister who will perform a three-way wedding, I'll consider it."

Surprise! They had already made arrangements. About three hours later, when we were all covered in cum and the room reeked of sex, there was a knock at the door. I expected Joe to ignore it, as he ordinarily would do when the phone or anything else interrupted our sex. Instead, he said, "That must be her, now."

I was confused, until he went to the door and admitted an attractive woman in a long white robe embroidered with quasi-religious symbols. "This is Reverend Delilah," he said. "She's here to marry us, if you're willing."

I shrugged. "Sure, why not?" I said. I still thought this might be part of an elaborate joke. It wasn't.

Reverend Delilah was ordained by one of those mail-order churches and specialized in performing unconventional weddings. With the three of us nude and stinking of mass fucking, she began the wedding ritual. "Dearly beloved . . ." I guess you know the rest of the words. When she reached the point where brides and grooms make their vows, Peter stood behind me and put his cock between my ass cheeks as he had done that very first night. Joe stood in front of me and placed the tip of his hard-on at the opening of my pussy. They both entered me, and the three of us stood tied together that way as we all said, "I do."

Reverend Delilah pinched each of our asses and intoned in mock seriousness, "By no legal authority whatsoever, I now pronounce you men and wife. Feel free to fuck the bride." When she left, we finished the fuck we had begun.

The wedding ceremony had no legal validity, but we live together as though it did. We all share the same bed. When I'm out with them, they both introduce me as their wife. I introduce them both as my husbands. People suppose we're joking, and we let it go at that. But we really do feel married. I'll always remember Joe's promise to let me go if I ever feel bored with them. It's very liberating to know that I have that option. It's been several years, though, and it doesn't look like I ever will. You might say we're as happy as three bugs in a rug.

I'm not the youngster I once was, but I'm still having the time of my life with my two husbands. The sex is great, and I'm enjoying our relationship as much as I ever did. Maybe, someday, the honeymoon will end, but I doubt it.

Now, tell me the truth. Is ours the weirdest erotic lifestyle you've heard about? If you've heard stranger ones, I guess I'll just have to read your book.

ME AND MY WIFES

On a visit to one of our favorite cities, we noticed Job and his family sitting at a table near ours. Even seated, it is obvious that Job is a big man, at least six-foot-two and weighing somewhere around two hundred pounds. His shoulders are broad. His hands are rough and callused. His face is tanned. Beside him, Neda and Wendy appear slight, almost birdlike. Both women are pale and thin. Neda is blond, while Wendy has red hair and freckles. Otherwise, their appearances are rather similar, their pinched faces demonstrating lives of hard work. What caught our attention was the fact that two of the children at the table called Neda "Ma," while the other one used that form of address on Wendy, but all three referred to Job as "Pa." After we struck up a conversation with them, Job joined us at our table. We began by asking what the relationship between him and the women was called.

We don't call it nothin'. We live out in the country, miles away from here. Us and our neighbors don't ask a bunch of questions. We mostly know how to mind our own business, but we take care of each other when somebody needs help. It was takin' care of neighbors that brung us together.

See, me and Wendy been married quite a few years. We were happy enough, I guess, even though we didn't have no kids. Weren't for failin' to try. I'm a healthy man and I need to get me some regular, just like I need to eat. Wendy didn't care all that much for sexin', but she knew her duty. Any time I was needin', she'd roll over and let me give her a poke. Only lasted a minute or two and kept me satisfied, pretty much. Just never took, I guess, 'cause even with all that breedin', we didn't have no kids.

Now Neda, on the other hand, she had her first just a little while after she moved in with ol' Skip. Poor little guy wasn't more'n eight months old when Skip went down. Skip's farm is right next to mine. Our families always was tight, and me and Skip grew up together. So when he got sick, me and Wendy started goin' over to see them every evenin' after workin'. Doc said it was cancer and wasn't much could be done for 'im.

Pretty soon, it got so Skip couldn't work his place no more, and I had to get the crop in for him. Wasn't long before he died. Poor Neda was all alone, 'cept for the baby. So it was natural for us to take care of her. We started by helpin' her work the place. After a while, it seemed foolish to keep two households going, so she and little Skip moved in with us. Our house ain't big, but there was room for the baby's crib. It was summer, so Neda just bedded down on a blanket in the kitchen.

Before long, the nights started gettin' chilly. Don't make much sense to keep the fire going at night, when you can just throw on another blanket. Couldn't ask Neda to keep sleepin' on that cold wooden floor in the kitchen, so she just moved into the bed with me and Wendy. The two ladies felt kind of funny about lyin' next to each other in bed, so I slept in the middle.

It was just for warmth at first. Neda would always stall for a bit before comin' to bed so I'd have a chance to poke Wendy's bunny in private. Then one night, while I was sleepin', I felt a woman's hand touchin' around my belly, lookin' for my johnnie. I knew it couldn't be Wendy. She never done that in her life. I was still half asleep, but johnnie came full awake and said, Okay let's do this thing.

Next thing I knew, Neda was under me. Man, she's really different from Wendy. First off, them titties. Wendy's got little tight ones, kinda pointy. But Neda. Wow, she's got udders, real big, round, and soft. I was holdin' and bobblin' them in my hands, just havin' a grand ol' time. Then there's the way she moved. Wendy always laid there, just lettin' me have my way. But Neda really wanted it. She wrapped her legs 'round me, sort of like tyin' me right in, like she was afraid I might pull out.

When I stuck johnnie in her little rabbit, she rose up to meet him. It was like she was gobblin' me up, suckin' johnnie in very deep like she really was glad to have him in there. Every time I slammed down to drive him in, she lifted her belly up to slap against mine and sort of rolled around in a little circle, givin' him the ride of his life. I was gruntin' like a boar, and she was makin' some pretty hot little noises herself.

I don't ever remember goin' that long before. It was feelin' so good, I just didn't want it to end. She didn't neither. Whenever johnnie got ready to spit, she seemed to know it. She'd change speed and direction to give him a little break. Then, when I had control over him again, she'd go back to slammin' up at me. I knew Wendy had to be awake by now, but it didn't matter. This was just too damn good. After a while, it seemed so natural, I didn't even think about it. I just let it happen.

Finally, there wasn't no way I could control it at all. I knew I was goin' to spout. After all them years of not havin' no babies with Wendy, I didn't even think none about that. I just let it go, pumpin' myself into Neda until she was filled with my syrup. Something strange happened. At least it seemed strange to me then.

Neda started makin' the same kind of sounds I was makin'. By God, that woman was gettin' off with me. I never really knowed a woman could do that. Man, it was somethin'. It always felt great when I let it go inside Wendy, but this was a whole lot better, 'cause the gal was getting pleasure from it too.

When we was both done, I rolled off and laid there on my back between the two women, tryin' to catch my breath. Neda didn't say nothin'. She just rolled over, with her back to me and went back to sleep, like that poke was what she was needin' and now that she had it, she could go about her business. I liked that idea and was thinkin' about it as I dozed off.

After a while, though, I felt a woman's hand fumblin' with johnnie again. I couldn't believe Neda could be ready again, but what the heck, if she was, I guess I could be too. Johnnie came up before I did, but when I was full awake I realized it wasn't Neda's hand. It was Wendy's. By God, that was a new one. She never, ever started the sexin'. I couldn't believe it. If she wanted it, though, it was my job to give it to her. So I did.

Man, that was the second surprise of the night. Wendy was hot. Ever bit as hot as Neda'd been. She really wanted it. She put my hands on her little titties and started playin' with johnnie, even more than Neda had. For the first time ever, she got up on top of me. It felt kind of strange bein' on the bottom, like a girlie, but I was so startled by the way she was takin' matters into her own hands that I just let her have her way.

She took hold of johnnie and put him right in her hole. She was hot and wet like I'd never known her to be. I just slipped right in without the least bit of a struggle. When I was buried in there, she started to move. I didn't have to do nothin'. I just lay there and let her do all the work. I could feel her draggin' her bunny up and down on my stick, givin' it a real workout. Usually, I would pop off inside Wendy as quick as can be, but that time, it went on for a good long doin'. Maybe because I had used some of it up on Neda just a little bit ago, or maybe because this was such a new experience that I wanted it to last.

Anyways, it kept up pretty good, with her ridin' me like I was her little pet pony and me reachin' up to play with her pointy tits. She was even moanin', soft and musical. I was like a rootin' boar that found his way to hog heaven. From the corner of my eye, I could see Neda lyin' on her side facin' us, takin' it all in. I didn't know if this night was goin' to change things between us all, but I couldn't think about that now. I was goin' to come again.

Then I did. The second one that night was even better than the first time with Neda. Every spurt seemed to start down deep in my stones and work its way up through the tubes like a whirlwind, spin-nin' around and makin' my head spin with it. To make it more unbe-lievable, Wendy's little bunny started doin' them things Neda's had done. She got all tight on johnnie's neck and seemed to open and close 'round him, pulling and squeezin' like on a cow's teat. Oh, it was good. She was sayin' somethin' about, "Job, I'm there. I'm there. I'm there."

The rest is kind of a blur, 'cept I can tell you it was the most sen-sational thing I ever felt before. Sexin' was always somethin' I needed, but this raised it to a whole 'nother level. It felt so danged good I never wanted it to end. Till it did. Then I was ready for it, all towed out and needin' sleep more'n anything.

I remember wonderin', as I drifted off, whether Wendy had done that just to make sure I still loved her after givin' Neda the poke. I found out later that wasn't it. What it was, she said, was that watchin' me and Neda made her horny, like a nanny goat in season. Now here's the best part. She's been that way ever since.

What happened is that her and me and Neda kept right on sleepin' together in that big ol' bed of ours. Sometimes I give it to

Neda. Sometimes I give it to Wendy. I see from that look on your face that you're wonderin' if I ever give it to both of them at the same time. I'll tell you this: I sure don't and never will. That would be sick. We ain't perverts.

What we are is one big happy family. I'm raisin' little Skip like he was my own. Neda got pregnant again pretty soon and we had little Ruthie, over there. Just before she was born, Wendy told us she was expectin', too. And along came Judah. The little ones got two different mamas but just the one daddy.

'Course, me and Neda can't get married. That would be against the law. Far as we're concerned—all six of us, I mean—I'm married to both of them. They get along just fine. Neither one of them mind it when I'm pokin' the other one. Fact, they both like watchin' me do it to each other. The sexin' is better than ever and gettin' better still every night. Most nights, I get 'em both. I even get one or the other of 'em some afternoons, when I come in for dinner.

We can't help comin' to town every few months. But you can have your big-city life. Me and my wifes are happy livin' just the way we do.

6

I CAN'T
STOP
LOOKING

OF ALL THE ACTIVITIES THAT TURN PEOPLE ON,
voyeurism is probably the most common. Many people use the
word "voyeurism" to refer to sneaky peeking or observing others
without their knowledge. According to most dictionaries, however,
the label can be given to the act of deriving erotic pleasure from seeing the sexual organs or sexual behavior of others.

Just about all of us experience some voyeuristic excitement in our
own relationships. We enjoy seeing our mates nude or in abbreviated
clothing. We tend to regard the resulting arousal as part of the process of foreplay. For the people in this chapter, voyeurism is an
important part of an erotic lifestyle.

Dane, who makes his living providing a venue for voyeurs, is married and conducts his voyeuristic activities with the approval and
even the assistance of his wife. He says she is a practical person who
doesn't care who warms him up as long as he comes home to her. On
occasions, she has even suggested that he stop at a peep show on the
way home from work to get his mojo working, knowing it will leave
him hot to trot and hard all night for her.

For Sue, on the other hand, visual stimulation is not merely foreplay but an end in itself. After her divorce, she was sexually frustrated

until she discovered that voyeurism could be the answer to her problem. She says watching other people have sex while satisfying her own erotic needs through masturbation is a substitute for having a partner of her own.

RESORT

Sue is thirty-six years old and in terrific shape. She runs six miles every day, which helps keep her trim and healthy. She has an athletic appearance, with a firm body and muscular arms and legs. Her blond curly hair is short, framing her heart-shaped face. Sue has light brown eyes and beautiful long eyelashes that almost reach her brows. She is just under five feet five inches tall but at first glance looks taller. As we get started, she appears shy and somewhat uncomfortable, but she soon settles in and becomes more open. She tells us she used to be in middle management, but recently she had a change in occupation.

My life did a complete turnabout last year when my husband shocked me with the news that he wanted a divorce. He said he met another woman, fell in love with her, and wanted out of our marriage. Until that point, I really thought things were going well. Certainly, our sex life was good. At least I thought it was. I've always been a little bit shy, but when it came to sex with my husband, I was ready, willing, and able to give it my all.

When I asked him if sex was the problem, if he thought our marriage was lacking sexually, he said that sex was probably the only thing holding it together for as long as it did. We'd been married for ten years before he decided he no longer wanted to be my husband. Needless to say, I was quite depressed for months on end.

Soon after my husband moved out of our house, I got more bad news. My mom's sister had passed away. We were always quite close.

She was in her late sixties, never married, and I was her only living relative, aside from my mom. She left her entire estate to me.

My aunt had owned and operated a resort, catering mostly to honeymoon couples. It was financially lucrative and allowed her to live in a beautiful parklike environment. There were thirty acres with lush manicured lawns, beautiful fruit trees, magnificent gardens, and a huge lake for swimming, fishing, and boating, all in a lovely country setting. There were twenty-six cottages on the property, along with a large restored Victorian house that my aunt had lived in and had spent a lot of money refurbishing.

My first thought was to sell it, but my mom had a different idea. She suggested I sell my house in the city instead and actually run the resort. The more I thought about it, the better I liked the idea. It would allow me to get away from my old life. It would give me something to do besides being depressed and would introduce me to a totally different lifestyle.

It turned out to be the best thing that I could have done. I was no longer a salaried employee in a high-rise office building in the city, but the owner of a thriving resort business. My life took on a whole new and better meaning. I no longer missed my married life or my ex-husband.

The only thing I did miss was sex. I had no one to share my passions with, and it left me feeling frustrated. There are a few singles resorts in the area, and I did consider visiting some of the bars and cocktail lounges in them, but the thought of getting into the dating scene intimidated me. I just couldn't bring myself to do it.

I don't mind telling you that I have masturbated all my life. I consider it a healthy form of release. But lying alone in my bed and stroking my vulva and clitoris just didn't give me what I was needing. I'm sure lots of divorced women have gone through the same thing and experienced the same disheartened appetite.

I tried keeping myself busy decorating my new house and adjusting to my new surroundings. All the cottages on the property were fairly new, with lots of glass. Every one faced the lake and had picture windows on three sides to maximize the views. Each of the units consisted of a large room furnished with a king-size bed, large dresser, sofa, some chairs, and a small refrigerator. Twelve of the cottages had hot tubs right in the rooms. Naturally, they rented at a higher price than the others. We don't have a restaurant on the premises, but there are several just up the road.

I soon discovered that running the resort did not require much in the way of hard work. There were two maids who cleaned and prepared the cottages for guests, a full-time gardener who came every day to keep up the grounds, a part-time clerk to help in the office, and a local handyman for odd jobs around the place. I didn't have much to do and so I took advantage of my leisure. After the first few weeks, I settled in completely and was able to sit back, relax, and soak up the sun while lying in a chaise longue in the private garden in back of my house.

One afternoon, as I sat in the garden, I noticed a young couple necking in the cottage nearest the house. They were in the hot tub, passionately hugging and kissing each other. I was sitting behind a rosebush, hidden from their view. They stayed for some time in each other's arms and kissed deeply. Then the woman stood up, and I had a clear and unobstructed view of her naked body. She was beautiful, and so was her youthful body. Her breasts stood out firm and straight, with pink nipples that were tall and hard. No sagging at her age. Her hips flared wide, accentuating her narrow waist. Her skin was creamy white, contrasting with the thatch of dark pubic hair that covered her mound.

I couldn't tear my eyes off of her. Now, try and understand this. I'm not sexually interested in women. I was turned on, but not by seeing her. It was the idea of looking into their window without their knowing it. The fact that I was catching them in a private intimate moment was getting to me. I felt a twinge between my legs and reached down to touch myself through the shorts I was wearing.

The man in the tub was looking up at her as he sat in the hot bubbly water. He was saying something to her, but of course I couldn't make it out. I watched as he started to caress her leg. Slowly, his hand moved up until it stopped at her hairy mound. She helped him by spreading her thighs apart to give him better access. His hand played with her pubes for a while. Then his finger parted her vaginal lips and disappeared inside. I imagined hearing passionate cries of joy as I watched her face and mouth contorting. Her hips rocked from side to side and back and forth in the motion of intercourse until she seemed to collapse in orgasm.

Watching them had such an impact on me that I wasn't at all aware that I was masturbating. My hand seemed to have a mind of its own, grinding the material of my shorts into my vulva, pulling it tight against my clit. I think I came at the same time she did. Even though I was all alone, I felt embarrassed and a little ashamed. I looked furtively around, anxious that someone might have caught me peeping. Then, sheepishly, I went into the house and took shelter in my own bedroom.

I sat there for a long time, thinking about what had happened. Gradually, the feeling of shame went away. I had just experienced the best climax I'd had since my husband left me. I reflected on it and realized that watching the couple making love had acted as an aphrodisiac that lifted me to the same level of arousal as had sex with my ex-husband.

Voyeurism could be the answer to my problem. Watching other people have sex while satisfying my erotic needs through masturbation could be a substitute for having a partner of my own. I certainly felt fulfilled by the experience. In some ways the act of watching was even more exciting and more stimulating than sex had been with my ex. Suddenly, I was hungry for more.

In the next few days, I looked for every possible vantage point for observing couples who rented cottages from me. Also, I bought a pair of expensive binoculars. I discovered that sitting in a rowboat on the lake permitted me to see very clearly into several of the cottages. The sunroom of my house gave me an even better view of the cottage where I had seen the couple in the hot tub. I watched them every day for the rest of their stay. After they left, I resolved to save that cottage for the most attractive couples. I thought of it as "the special cottage."

Life became a series of voyeuristic experiences for me. I was very careful that no one could see me looking. I was watching live pornography all the time. At night, I would keep the lights off in my room so I could peer out of the dark into the cottages around me. I became so expert at masturbating that I could make my sessions take as little or as much time as I wanted. Watching was such a wonderful turn-on for me that it became all I could think about.

Just today, I had one of the best porno shows ever. An interracial couple arrived early this morning and said they wanted to rent a cottage for one day and night only. I usually have a three-day minimum, but there was something about them that told me to make an exception. While they were in the registration office, the woman was all over the man. She showed no embarrassment whatsoever. I couldn't actually see what she was doing, because they were hidden by the counter, but from the look on her partner's face, I'd guess she was rubbing his penis.

Naturally, I rented them the special cottage. As soon as our business was done, I locked up the office and went to the sunroom of my house. I closed the drapes and hid behind them so I could freely look into their glass room and watch everything that went on. As soon as they entered the room and closed the door behind them, the woman climbed all over him. She practically tore his clothes off and proceeded to quickly remove hers. There was no doubt that she was the aggressor and was in control of their sexual rendezvous.

The woman was attractive and looked to me in her mid-thirties. The man she was with appeared an awful lot younger than she. It was obvious that they were not honeymooning, but there for a one-night adventure. She was rather fleshy, but extremely sensuous. Her chocolate-colored breasts were large with big black areolae circling her erect nipples. They, too, were quite large, standing out firm and straight in front of her.

Just looking at the two of them and anticipating what I was about to see their naked bodies do made me feel all hot and oozy. I think I was even more turned on looking at her nakedness than at his. She had a big round ass that was very prominent and stood out from her body. She paraded around the room, showing off her body and getting her friend all turned on.

He looked as though he was hypnotized by her. I could almost see his eyes burn as the temptress danced erotically for him. His cock was so hard and long, I could see it clearly even without the binoculars I was holding. He touched it every now and then while she teased him with her alluring sexual gestures. She was licking her lips and showing him her open mouth. Her tongue slowly moved in and out in an obscenely suggestive motion while her eyes danced up and down his naked body.

I watched every move they made, and the more I watched the more excited I got. I took off my clothes and let my own nakedness excite me further. My nipples were hard as rocks, and my vagina was getting wetter and wetter. I was experiencing sex vicariously through them, and it was more of a turn-on than you can imagine. I didn't even have to touch myself anywhere to feel sexual pleasure. Watching them was making me tingle. That woman was sex personified. I've never seriously considered sex with another woman, but if I ever did, I would want it to be with someone like her.

She pulled a chair into the middle of the room and pointed for him to sit down in it. I think I gasped audibly when I saw her naked body straddle his. She sat on his lap, her back to him, her legs spread wide on each side of his. Before she was completely seated on him, she reached for his penis and buried it inside her. I watched through my binoculars as his erection disappeared inside her womb. Next to her, his skin seemed deathly pale and colorless.

She rocked up and down real slowly, each time giving me a peek as his swollen member went in and out of her. Her body moved back and forth against his penis. Whenever I caught a glimpse of it, I was sure I could see it sparkling with fluid. She placed one of his hands on each of her heaving breasts and licked her lips with her tongue. As his hands filled with the flesh of her breasts, I could see her nipples growing longer and harder.

As I stared at her body, and especially at her breasts, I could feel my own nipples aching for attention. Slowly, I started to fondle them. I love the sensation of watching other people having sex while gratifying my own erotic needs. As I squeezed and played with my erect nipples, I watched the young man doing the same to his partner.

I could tell from the expression she wore that she was moaning and groaning with pleasure. Her body moved harder and faster with each stroke of his fingers. My binoculars made everything close and clear. It was as though I were in the same room with them. I could see beads of perspiration on her breasts. I felt I could count the number of little bumps on her dark areolar disks. I focused on her nipples just as her lover started to roll them between his thumbs and forefingers.

They became so erect that it sent chills down my spine. I watched his lips pucker as his tongue darted in and out of her ear. This seemed to make her nipples even bigger and harder. With one hand I held my binoculars and with the other I began satisfying the urgent need I was feeling in my vagina.

I pushed my finger in and out and felt my juices flowing. Still watching the couple through the window, I continued pleasing myself, my finger moving from deep inside me to my pulsing clitoris. With the fluid that flowed from my womb, I gingerly lubricated my clit. I was getting closer and closer to a point of orgasm.

I could see them rocking together to the rhythms of preorgasmic sex. Then, suddenly, the voluptuous woman stopped abruptly and got up from his lap. I watched his penis slide out of her, soaked with the juices of her sex. I felt my own wetness with my fingers, hoping they weren't finished. I was soooo close.

She was far from done, though. Quickly, she placed both her hands on the footrail of the bed and bent over it, giving me a full view of her from behind. I watched as she spread her legs wide, pulling her buttocks apart and parting her labia. She said something to her partner, and he moved behind her. He stood poised with one hand on his penis. Slowly, he slid it into her vagina and it disappeared into her depths.

Once inside her, he put hands on her hips to guide her movements as he glided in and out. I watched his young body gyrating slowly as he drove his erect penis firmly into her and eased it out again. She was moving her hips and bottom in circles to accommodate his strokes. Every now and then I could get a glimpse of his wet penis pumping in and out of her. Seeing them in this position made me feel hotter. I had an even better view than before.

They were moving faster now, and his hands were playing with her hanging breasts. She held the bedrail firmly and moved her body in perfect harmony with his. I imagined I could hear her screams of ecstasy from the confines of my home. Watching the two copulating so furiously brought on my own orgasm. I rubbed my naked vulva hungrily until I was transported into a sexual paradise. My eyes closed tightly while my orgasm washed over me. Then I opened them again and looked at the lovers in the cottage next door.

I was sure I was seeing them reach their climaxes now. I watched his muscular buttocks tighten and loosen as he pumped. They bucked and heaved until I saw his deflated penis slip out from inside her oozing vagina. She stood straight up then, turned around to face her partner, and embraced him for a long, long time. They kissed and hugged until they both lay on the bed exhausted. After that, I took a nap, only to wake up and watch them make another go at their lustful passions. The three of us came twice more before they stopped making love and I stopped watching.

I have seen so many couples having sex that I think I could write a book on it. It has become an important and fulfilling part of my life since I've been alone. I have become a lot more knowledgeable about sex. When the time is right, and I meet the right person, I know I'll be a better lover and make my partner a more sexually satisfied person. Until then, I won't become desperate. I'm very happy to watch and observe and keep myself sexually content.

PEEP SHOW

Dane is in his early fifties, with silver hair to prove it. His steely gray eyes peer through wire-rimmed bifocals. He wears a neatly trimmed mustache and goatee, which give him an air of dignity. When we meet with him in the office at the back of his business establishment, he is wearing a blue pin-striped suit and conservative tie. He is on the short side, just about five-foot-seven, and slightly built, with narrow shoulders and hips. His executive bearing seems mildly inconsistent with his occupation.

I haven't always been a flesh peddler. I used to be a highly respected engineer. If we signed our work the way artists do, my name would appear on quite a few highway overpasses and other transportation projects all over the country, not to mention several in the Middle East. Things started falling apart when the economy took a downturn, though. I don't mean the things I engineered. They'll never fall apart. I mean my career.

I had been a man on the way up ever since I entered the work world. I started at the bottom with a well-known engineering firm as soon as I got my degree. I began distinguishing myself right away. After a few years, I was put in charge of several small projects. When I had proven myself that way, my assignments started getting bigger and more important.

I was sent overseas quite a bit, but most of the time I was in the home office in New York City. I grew up in the Midwest, but I really came to love the Big Apple. There was always something happening. A person could always satisfy his needs, no matter what they happened to be. Mine ran to voyeurism.

When I was a little kid, I used to peek in a neighbor's window to watch her undressing. The thrill it gave me stayed with me. In New York, I discovered peep shows. Oh, I loved going into those places. Let me describe them for you.

Outside would be a big sign that said LIVE NUDE GIRLS. Inside it was always somewhat dark and sleazy-looking. There would be a series of little booths, smaller than a phone booth. I'd go into one of them to get warmed up.

There would be a little window in front of me with a curtain covering it from the other side. I'd put coins or tokens in a slot and the curtain would open for a measured interval—probably forty-five seconds, but it seemed like less. On the other side was a little stage with two or three girls gyrating their naked bodies. They were called dancers, but they made no pretext of dancing. They just moved in as sexual a fashion as possible, grinding their hips in a way that displayed their vaginas and made their boobs bounce.

A man could hold a couple of dollars up in front of the window to have one of the girls come up and gyrate right in front of him. First, of course, she'd reach over the top of the partition to grab the money. She'd wiggle specially for him, or even put her foot up on a rail under the window so he could jerk off to a close-up view of her open vulva. Better be quick, though, because that curtain would close as soon as the time was up and you'd have to pay again for another look.

For that reason, I didn't usually tip the dancers to get a close-up. I liked to be a little more leisurely in my pleasures. So after the show got me hard, I'd head for a one-on-one booth. Some of the places called them "conversation booths," although I can assure you that conversation had very little to do with what went on inside them.

The conversation booths were a little bigger than those others. Now, I can tell you the exact size—four by eight feet. A floor-to-ceiling pane of glass divides it into two four-foot-square compartments. I'd be in one of them and a nude girl would be in the other, on a cut-off mattress that filled her entire space. I'd pass anywhere from five to twenty dollars to her through an opening in the glass, and then the fun would begin.

I could go through the motions of telling her what I wanted to see, but let's face it, all men want the same thing. After a while, I realized I didn't have to tell her anything to get what I came for. She'd spread her legs wide to show me her open vagina. Then she'd rub her breasts and play with her nipples while stroking her vaginal lips and clitoris.

I'd remove my pants, hang them on a hook, and play with myself until I got off. The thrill came from watching her play with herself at the same time. If she was good, she'd pretend to have an orgasm. That would heighten my excitement, even though if I thought about it I had to realize that she put on this little performance maybe thirty or forty times a day and couldn't possibly have that many climaxes.

I really loved those one-on-one booths. The experience turned me on so much that I'd usually came within two or three minutes. Even after coming, I'd stay turned on for the rest of the day. Sometimes I'd go there on my lunch hour. Afterwards, as I went about my work, my mind would keep returning to the peep show and I'd find myself with an erection right there at my desk. I don't mind telling you there were plenty of times when I'd have to go to the men's room in the middle of the afternoon to relieve myself. I'd sit there with my pants down jerking off and reliving the experience I'd had with the girl in the booth.

It worked as a kind of tool to enhance my marriage. When I got home, I'd still be thinking about the girl I had seen that day. I'd jump on my wife as soon as I walked in the door. Sometimes I'd make love to her right on the living room floor. As I entered her, I'd be picturing the open vagina of the young lady who had entertained and titillated me earlier. As I caressed my wife's breasts, I'd be imagining the breasts of the girl in the booth.

Once my wife asked what had made me so frisky, and I told her all about it. She had no problem with it at all, because she realized that it improved our sex life at home. After all, there was a pane of glass between me and the girl. It wasn't like I was committing adultery or anything. There were even times when my wife was feeling particularly horny that she'd call me at work and suggest I stop off at the peep show on the way home. She knew that if I did, she could count on my being plenty hot to trot and staying hard for her all night long.

Places like that are only available in big cities, and not all big cities, either. About five years ago, when an influx of young fellows started making an impression with new concepts they were bringing from engineering schools, I began falling from my position of prominence in the company. They transferred me to their satellite office in this city. I felt awful about what I considered a demotion, and to make matters worse, there were no peep shows here.

I missed the diversion and the excitement, and so did my wife. Whenever I had reason to visit the home office in New York, I'd be sure and take advantage of those one-on-one booths. You may think of the Empire State Building and the Statue of Liberty as the big attractions there, but to me New York will always be sleaze city, the voyeurism capital of the world.

Two years ago, the ax fell. The company told me they were closing the office here, and there was no place for me. It was a euphemistic way of firing me. Naturally, they offered me a golden parachute—early retirement with a fat severance package. Still, I was devastated. At my age, jobs are not easy to find. I searched and consulted with headhunters, but found that it was hopeless.

I became depressed. I felt useless. I had no job, no place in the world, no reason to feel important. Income was a problem, too. Even if I invested the company's kiss-off, there would not be enough in dividends to live on. I felt so low that I couldn't even get it up anymore. My wife was understanding, but how much celibacy can a woman take? My impotence made me even more depressed, and of course that made me more impotent. My wife suggested I go to a peep show to get turned on for her, but there just weren't any in this town.

One of my former colleagues suggested I start my own engineering business. At first the idea pleased me. If I had my own business, nobody could ever fire me again. I'd make all the decisions. I'd be master of my own financial destiny. As I thought about it, however, I realized I wouldn't have a chance going up against the larger firms with their big staffs and glitzy setups. No, I would need to come up with some other idea for a business.

Then it hit me. Why couldn't I open up a peep show establishment?

I'd be my own boss, make lots of money, and give this town something it desperately needed. Best of all, I'd be able to get myself all the sex shows a man could handle. When I mentioned the idea to my wife, she was all for it. She didn't say why, but I realized my limp penis had something to do with it. She's a practical woman. She doesn't care who warms me up as long as I come home to her.

It took some time battling with the city government and quite a few promises on my part about keeping the place upscale, but we finally were able to open our doors. I leased what used to be a carpet store and spent quite a bit of money renovating the interior to set up the necessary booths. The exterior is pretty conservative as these things go. No neon. No banners proclaiming LIVE NUDE GIRLS. Just a quiet sign that says VIEWS OF NIRVANA.

I think the part I liked best was hiring the staff. I even had my wife help out. We were both surprised at how many pretty young women answered our ads. My wife would interview them first and do the preliminary screening, eliminating those she didn't think were sexy enough. She seems to have very good judgment in that regard.

The ones who passed her cut would then go into a one-on-one booth with me to demonstrate how they would perform for a customer. I'd act like the customer, even jerking off while watching them. My wife knew that, and it was all right with her. Especially since it got my mojo working again. From the moment the job interviews began, our sex life at home was right back on track.

Within months, the money started coming in. The girls pay me so much per shift to work here, and then split their take with me, fifty-fifty. As you've seen, we sell books, videos, sex toys, and other paraphernalia out front. I'm earning more money running this place than I ever made as a top engineer. Ironic, isn't it?

Best of all, I have to make sure the girls are doing a good job and keeping me within the promises I made to the city. So I visit each of them in their booths at least once a week. They are supposed to perform for me the same way they do for a customer, which is the role I play during these employee evaluations. To make it authentic, I even masturbate like a customer when I'm in the booth. Heh, heh. Just being a diligent employer.

Making a good living makes me feel like a man again. So does my returned ability to get erections. I think I have more of them and keep them up longer than I ever did before. More important, Views of Nirvana gives me the opportunity to indulge my erotic lifestyle by catering to my penchant for voyeurism.

7

MEN WHO
LOVE MEN

SAME-SEX EROTICISM HAS BEEN PRACTICED AMONG
men throughout recorded history. In some societies and at some
times, it has been regarded as a perfectly acceptable behavior. Else-
where and at other periods of history, it has been treated as an
offense against law and morality, sometimes punishable by death in
the most horrible ways imaginable. Although it came to a different
conclusion in 2003, in 1973, the United States Supreme Court held
that a Florida law forbidding "the abominable and detestable crime
against nature" was a valid prohibition of sexual conduct between
males. The court said that the phrase had a long enough history to
be intelligible to anyone who took the trouble to determine its
meaning.

Legal implications aside, there can be no doubt that the use of
such language is an expression of society's official position. Man-to-
man sex is a crime against nature. Even more significant, it is the one
crime that is distinguished from all others by being abominable and
detestable. No court ever said that about John Wayne Gacy's serial
murders of more than thirty victims, or even about the 2001 attack
on the World Trade Center in New York City.

Reading the stories in this chapter makes it hard to understand how that phrase can be applied to the behavior of the people who tell them. Mason, a physician, has dedicated his life to helping patients with cancer. Armando, a cook, enjoys giving outsiders a taste of the foods of his native Puerto Rico. Their personalities differ in that Mason is devoted to a single partner, while Armando likes playing the field. What their erotic lifestyles have in common is that both find comfort in the arms of other men.

PARTNERS FOR LIFE

Mason is thirty-four years old. He is of medium height, with a slender body and delicate features. His thick black hair is cut to flatter his lean, sculptured face. His gray eyes complement his newly acquired sunburn. Mason speaks in a low, soft voice, gesturing with his graceful hands and long, tapering fingers. He wears a serious expression, not smiling very often. When he talks about his partner, though, his face brightens and his eyes sparkle.

I'm a medical oncologist, and most of my time is spent helping my cancer patients stay alive. It's hard for me to be casual or light-hearted, because I am so emotionally involved with life and death. I've always had a serious nature. Maybe that is why I chose to be a doctor. I've always taken my sexual relationships seriously, too. I don't know if I can say that I have an erotic lifestyle. Let's just say there is plenty of sex in my life. I'm homosexual.

As far back as I can remember, I knew I was different. I wasn't like most of my childhood friends who played with guns and liked hitting each other. I didn't enjoy their rough and tumble games and I didn't like getting into fights, not even play fights. I preferred the company of girls my age, rather than boys. Adults used to wink and whisper about what a Casanova I was and what a ladies' man I would be when I grew up. But by the time I was eight or nine, I found myself sexually aroused by the sight of a man's penis.

When I was a youngster, my mother used to take me to the beach with her. I remember how much I enjoyed sitting in the sun and looking at the men in tight-fitting bathing suits. I would try to picture their penises and imagine how big they would be if not held down by their bathing suits. My father died when I was just a baby, but I had seen grown men's penises in public restrooms. I remember wondering whether mine would ever be that massive.

On those visits to the beach, I fell madly in love with the handsome lifeguards. All of them. They looked so perfectly manly to me. They were always beautifully tanned, with strong muscular bodies. The effect they had on me even then was definitely sexual. I can still remember how aroused it made me to watch them strut or just sit in their elevated chairs towering high above the rest of us. Even in my preteen years, I would be conscious of my erection when one of them chanced to look in my direction. I'll admit that, even now, there is something about a lifeguard that still turns me on.

As I got older, I dated a few women, more to please my mother than because I really wanted to. I think she was aware that I was different and believed I would change if only I met the right woman. But, of course, that never happened. I just wasn't at all attracted to females. I tried having sex with them, but it never really felt right. Most of the time, I wouldn't even be capable of erection with them. When I was, I was not able to reach orgasm. I never went to bed with the same woman twice, because after the first time, they would want nothing further to do with me.

It could not have been otherwise, because I was attracted only to men. It wasn't until I left home for college and got away from the supervision of my mother that I stopped trying to be what I was not and stopped going out with women altogether. At first, that meant I had almost no social life at all. I knew I wasn't really interested in women, but I wasn't emotionally ready to start experimenting sexually with men. Somewhere in my junior year, I had a brief groping episode with another male student and experienced my first orgasm that was not self-induced.

He and I were both too embarrassed to repeat the incident, but it did make me finally understand the difference between me and heterosexual men. Until then, I knew I wasn't asexual, because I masturbated frequently. But I hadn't understood that I was homosexual. To me, homosexuals had seemed an alien group. I thought they all swished and waved limp wrists at each other while dressing in women's clothing. That's probably what you think, too. Well, maybe not you, because you are sex researchers and know a little more than most people do. But that does seem to be the general attitude toward gay men. Even the word "gay" has a suggestion of flamboyance about it.

As you can see, there's nothing flamboyant about me. Personally, as well as politically, I'm quite conservative. Even after I realized what I was, I found it difficult to come out. I didn't pretend to be straight, as some men in my position do. On the other hand, I didn't flaunt my homosexuality, either. I've know men who, upon discovering their nature, have gone through a series of same-sex partners, one after another, the way athletes change their socks. That's just not me.

I developed a few close friendships that had sexual aspects to them and experimented with my newfound homosexuality, but I was always careful. It goes without saying that I practiced safe sex. The same fascination with sickness that brought me to the medical profession makes me terrified of getting a horrible and fatal sexually transmitted disease, so I wouldn't even touch another man's penis unless he was wearing a condom.

More important, I stayed away from the looseness and promiscuity that seems to characterize young homosexual men. I wasn't and didn't want to be one of those guys who go from one partner to the next. I certainly didn't sleep with every man with whom I shared an evening. I had to know him and feel a connection before I would even consider having sex.

I guess I was looking for Mr. Right. It wasn't until I was nearly finished with med school that I found Jeffrey. He turned out to be the love of my life. Jeffrey was working in the men's clothing department at a high-end department store. His personality was outgoing, without being outrageous. The complete opposite of mine. He was louder, more gregarious, and friendly with everyone. He was always laughing and joking, the kind of person everyone likes. Men and women.

The first time I met Jeffrey was in the store where he worked. I had decided to buy a new suit, but was not very knowledgeable about fashion. I walked into the men's clothing department and just stood there, looking around and feeling a sense of bewilderment. I didn't even know how to begin. Jeffrey sensed that as he approached me and offered assistance. He helped me pick out something conservative to go with my personality, but at the same time fashionable. He knew about every designer in the business, referring to them as if they were personal friends.

He knew in advance what would look right on me. He ended up dressing me from the tip of my toes to the top of my head. He spoke with authority about which styles complimented my body shape and skin color, and which ones I definitely should not wear. I felt like a million dollars in the clothes he selected for me, so I turned myself over to him completely and bought whatever he recommended. I felt myself attracted to him powerfully. Right after my fitting, we made plans for dinner that night.

Jeffrey and I had one thing very much in common. Neither of us was flighty. Neither of us slept around. Neither of us took sex or our sexuality lightly. I was pleased to learn that he had been in a serious relationship for several years before I met him. He and his partner had lived together from the time he was in his early twenties until a tragic car accident took his partner's life. They had been faithful to each other. They had been in love. This made me feel safe with Jeffrey as our relationship developed.

Jeffrey knew everything I did not. He taught me how to dress, where to get my hair styled, where the restaurants were that were good but didn't cost a fortune. Most important, he infected me with some of his optimism. When I saw the glass half empty, he showed me that it was half full. When I felt sad, Jeffrey was always right there to cheer me up.

We moved slowly at first. We didn't jump into anything. We didn't even have sex until the fourth time we were out together. He was patient. I liked that about him, because I didn't want it to be all about sex and only about sex. I needed a partner who could talk to and listen to me. Someone who cared about who I was and what I wanted out of life. When we finally did have our first experience together, we turned out to be a perfect match. After that we became inseparable.

We have been together for nine years now. We both expect our relationship to last forever. We've talked about it and agreed that if our state recognized same-sex marriages, we'd get married in a New York minute. Recently, we bought an old brownstone building that we're having redone. For the past couple of months, Jeffrey and I have been eating and breathing our remodel. I'm excited about our new home, but not nearly as emotional about it as he. He is totally consumed with our house, and I am very happy that it makes him so excited. Jeffrey says he can't wait for our new bedroom to be completed, because the new atmosphere in the room will make our lovemaking all that more beautiful.

We have a very satisfying sex life. I credit that to the fact that we both aim to please. We care so very much for each other that giving sexual satisfaction to our mate is always a primary concern for each of us. Jeffrey loves to pamper me and especially enjoys bringing me to higher and higher levels of sexual fulfillment. Sometimes our lovemaking turns into hours of bliss.

If I should be feeling down, Jeffrey is always right there to take care of me and massage my troubles away. He loves getting me into the tub and bathing my entire body with fragrant oils and lotions. I positively die when he washes my hair and massages my scalp. I find this so very relaxing that it seems to transport me to another world.

It was Jeffrey's idea to buy a professional massage table, which we keep in our exercise room. We have given it a lot of use, taking turns giving and receiving pleasure. Jeffrey gives the most wonderful massage a person could ask for. His hands are soft, yet strong enough to make all the aches of a day's travail just melt away. The oils he pours onto my skin smell sweet and make me almost dizzy with their pungency. He can massage my feet for half an hour, rotating my toes and kneading his fingers into the soles and heels until I tingle with delight. Then his fingers work their way up the backs of my legs until I feel totally renewed. Jeffrey never rushes through anything that he does.

When my legs feel completely relaxed, he begins to work on my buttocks. I love feeling his fingers dig deep into the flesh, rolling it from side to side, until I achieve a semiconscious state. It never fails to give me an erection when his fingers dip into the crevasse between my buttocks. He strokes lightly, up and down the length of my crack, his fingertips lightly circling my anus until I'm groaning with delight. When he turns me over onto my back, my penis is hard and long. At that point, if it could talk it would be begging to be fondled.

Jeffrey is a master of genital massage. He caresses every millimeter of my sensitive organ with well-oiled fingers. He strokes and rubs it all over until it grows even longer. He knows when and where to apply a little pressure and exactly when and where to be gentle. When I'm coming close to orgasm, he knows it instinctively and he slows down. His hand will slide tenderly down to the base of my penis and then move to my scrotum, where, again, he knows how to apply just the right amount of pressure.

He is also a master of oral sex. When my excitement subsides just enough, his mouth closes over my penis, tenderly, lovingly. It always feels so safe and warm inside. He gives me a moment to adjust to the sensation and then begins to drive me crazy as his slithering tongue makes its way up and down the entire length of my shaft. I can feel the blood vessels pulsing through the sheath of my penis. Chills of sensation flood my body. Best of all, I love feeling the tip of his tongue moving around the corona at the base of my glans. With a delightful sensation of friction, I can feel droplets of preorgasmic fluid escaping from the opening of its tip.

Jeffrey can keep me just seconds away from an orgasm for hours at a time, always knowing when to back off and when to proceed. He covers my lips and my entire nude body with soft kisses. Then, when he senses that the time is right, he brings me to completion. He'll take my penis in his hand and lick it from top to bottom. With his other hand, he'll tenderly fondle my scrotum. When I'm poised on the brink of sexual elation, he swallows my erection, letting his mouth glide softly over its length. I am immediately ferried away into a world of libidinous bliss as my climax empties me into my lover's waiting throat.

When I return to earth, my orgasm spent, he lifts me off the table and carries me like a baby to our bed, where we lie together, embracing each other. It makes me feel safe and content in the arms of the person I love most. We hold each other tightly and lovingly as all the cares of life seem to fade away. I feel blessed to have found my soul mate, someone who will love, protect, and respect me for the rest of my life.

Our lifestyle may be unconventional by contemporary American standards, but homosexuality has existed from the beginning of time. Researchers estimate that somewhere between 10 and 20 percent of the population would be homosexual if they felt free to make a choice. That's a big chunk of humanity, so maybe the way we live isn't all that unusual after all. We don't hide who and what we are, but we don't feel any need to flaunt it, either.

I do wish, though, that people would be more accepting of lifestyles they perceive to be different than their own. There really is no scientific basis for discriminating against anyone because of a sexual preference. If only society would accept that everyone is different and entitled to be different, the world would be a happier place. But the times they are a-changin', and maybe as education improves, things will get better.

A LITTLE HELP FROM THE FAMILY

Armando was five years old when he left Puerto Rico to come and make a new home with his family in New York City. Now, at the age of twenty-three, he is a part owner in his family's restaurant business. He is about five feet eight inches tall with a small and slender body. His black shiny hair is thick and wavy, and he has dark brown eyes that blend with his olive skin. He is a high-energy person, constantly moving about and working quickly as he speaks with us. His voice is warm and personable, and his outgoing charm keeps us amused and entertained. His face wears a constant smile, flashing his straight white teeth, and he never seems to be at a loss for words. He has the slightest bit of a Caribbean Spanish accent.

I do a lot of the cooking for our restaurant. We serve the real McCoice here, home cooking from our beautiful Puerto Rico. My personal specialties are *arroz con gandules* and *papas rellenos*. The majority of people who eat here are Puertoriqueños, but we also get a lot of anglos who are curious to try our food. I'm pleased to tell you that many of those who tried it liked it enough to come back for more.

Now I know you didn't come here to eat, so I'll get right into my erotic lifestyle, what you asked me about. As you know, or maybe I should say as you can see, I'm gay. I don't hide that fact. I never did. When I was twelve years old I realized the reason I was different from my friends was because I was gay. I didn't keep it a secret from my parents. I came right out with it and told them I was. They told the rest of our family and friends, and pretty soon everyone knew. I've never been in that nasty old closet. My family let me be the person who I really am.

I share my life with my family. I think most Puerto Rican families are close. I know we are. They all accept and love me for what I am. So it is easy for me to be natural about my gay lifestyle. My oldest sister is about the same size as me and she never hesitates to ask me to try on a new dress or outfit to see how it looks. I'm not a cross-dresser, but I love trying on women's clothes. It's a real turn-on for me, and she knows it.

Sometimes I flirt with men who come into our restaurant. My family don't have any problem with that. They're amused by it. I got that gaydar, so I can always tell whether a man is gay or not. I don't come on to a guy who is straight. Myself, I'm rather flamboyant—you know, right out there—so it doesn't take a mental genius to know where I'm at. I have managed to live my lifestyle openly, without inhibitions or hidden desires. I don't hesitate to try and pick up a man when I feel attracted to him. I'm pleased to tell you I have fucked more men that came to eat at our restaurant than any others. I'm sure word gets around. Gay guys tend to hear things about each other.

My family is so open that they let all their curiosity come out. After I have a date with someone I met when they were around, they ask me questions like "Did you like him?" or "Will you be seeing him again?" The same kinds of questions they ask my sister when she goes out with a man. Just like they say to her, they are always telling me to settle down with one man and how they hope I find the right person soon. It's sweet. I'm pleased to tell you how wonderful it is for me to be able to be myself and not have to hide my feelings.

All the credit goes to my family for being such understanding and loving people. So far, I've never met another gay man who can really be himself and talk freely about his lovers in an open and honest conversation with his family. I am truly blessed that my family accepts unconditionally who I am. It's fun to be able to talk with them about who I find attractive, who I slept with, and what kind of man turns me on.

I'm sure they have concerns with health problems, but they have confidence in me to practice safe sex. I'm very careful about that. I won't even touch another man's dick unless he has a condom on. I carry them with me all the time, and if there's even the slightest chance of contact, I hurry up and put one on.

Last week, my mother actually set me up with a gorgeous young guy who came into the restaurant. I was running a little late, and she kept calling me on the phone to see what was keeping me. Finally, she just told me to hurry up and get my ass over there pronto. When

I asked her what was the rush, she said she couldn't keep this magnificent-looking man here much longer.

As soon as I arrived, my mama introduced me to the handsome stranger, saying, "I think you and Julio should go out together. I'll cover the kitchen, so you can leave early." Then she left me and Julio alone so we could make arrangements. Julio couldn't believe any of it. He just kept saying he wished he had a mama like mine.

After he left, every member of my family got into the act, pelting me with questions. "Where will you go? What are you going to wear? Did he seem like your type? Do you think he's good-looking?" Of course Mama's taking all the credit because she set me up with what she referred to as "The Adonis."

That night, Julio and I had dinner together and then went to a well-known gay bar in Greenwich Village. We drank and danced the night away. Julio was a great dancer and everyone at the bar took notice how graceful he was. When I started sensing that other men were coming on to him, I got a little uptight. He must have noticed, because he suggested we leave. We both were feeling our drinks and having a real good time. Julio invited me to his apartment a few blocks away. Hand in hand we strolled in the haze of our inebriation until he led me into his small studio.

Before I had a chance to look around or even sit down, Julio was all over me. Usually I'm the aggressor but Julio moved much faster than even me. He quickly slipped my clothes off and, before I knew it, we were both naked and jumping into the Murphy bed that he pulled down from the wall. Things were a little blurry, but we managed to slip on condoms in spite of that. First his hands played around with my cock, and then he asked me to do the same for him. It seemed like we masturbated each other for hours, but since we were so drunk, it's hard to tell.

Julio directed me onto my back and then climbed on top of me. We were in a sixty-nine position and sucking feverishly at each other's penis. I always loved doing sixty-nine, but I especially liked the way Julio did it. He was slow and methodical and took all efforts to bring me sensations that drove me wild. First he would lick my hard-on up and down and then he would gulp it deep into his throat until it felt like he was swallowing it all up.

I guess because we were both so stoned, it took us forever to orgasm. That made it even better. After a long, long time, we both shot our loads. We were so drunk that after we finally came, we both fell into a deep sleep. When we woke up early the next morning we got it on again. This time we were sober and could concentrate solely on our sex maneuvers.

Julio had woken up with his cock already hard. He stroked mine until it too jumped to attention. Then he turned toward a drawer next to the bed and opened it up. After rolling a condom onto each of us, he handed me a tube of lubricating jelly. "Would you rub this on my cock?" he said. "May I fuck you in the ass?" Usually most of the gay men I've been with don't ask. They just assume. I'm even guilty of that myself sometimes. I was a little turned on by Julio's politeness and proceeded to lubricate his hard-on.

He was very gentle with me and took his time to penetrate my anus. By the time his cock slid all the way inside, my ass had adjusted quite comfortably. He turned my body a little to one side, giving him enough room to grab on to my throbbing shaft. He masturbated me with his hand while he butt-fucked me with his penis. Julio kept up a steady movement with his hand on my cock, and his heaving body never missed a beat.

The room was soon filled with our cries of passion and moans of horny bliss. The two of us frolicked excitedly into oblivion until our orgasm was ready to release its gushing flow. I heard Julio panting, his labored breathing interrupted by the onset of his orgasm. With a strangled moan, he keened, "I'm coming, Armando, I'm coming in you." Next thing I know I'm coming too. The two of us spent most of the morning fucking each other's brains out until I had to leave for work.

The very second I stepped inside the restaurant, my whole family jumped in to ask how my date was. I had to answer a million and one questions for them. But who can complain when your family takes such an interest in you?

Julio and I were a couple for a few months, and then we went our separate ways. It didn't bother me, but I know my family was hoping that Julio would be the one and I would stop looking around. Someday, maybe. Right now, I like playing the field.

My mother is still always watching out for me, especially when a gay man comes into the restaurant. It is amazing how she can start up a conversation with a total stranger and talk about her gay son who is still searching for his life partner. I'm sure you must have talked with hundreds of gay men, but I bet you never met one whose family helps to set him up. I think that in itself makes my lifestyle as erotic as it can get.

8

WOMAN TO WOMAN

A PHILOSOPHICAL BATTLE IS CURRENTLY RAGING about whether the Old Testament should be seen as a poetic record of Western mythology or taken as a literal account of historical occurrences. We are going to stay out of that fray. There is no doubt, though, that the Bible tells us a great deal about how we view ourselves, our relationship to the universe, and certain questions of morality.

Although the laws of Leviticus specifically prohibit male homosexual conduct, there is nothing anywhere in the Old Testament that mentions same-sex contact between women. To us, this suggests that humans do not regard homosexuality among females with the same abhorrence as among males. Kinsey's research in the 1940s, and ours in the 1990s and the beginning of the twenty-first century, indicates the same. Although not as much social stigma is attached to gay men now as it was in the past, there has always been less disapproval directed at gay women.

This does not mean it is easy for a woman who desires sex with other women to admit that fact publicly, or even to face it herself. Diana, whose story is told in this chapter, did not find out that she was a lesbian until she was an adult and had already given up on ever finding sexual fulfillment. On the other hand, Umeko knew she was a lesbian from the time she was a preteenager and now takes an active and very public part in lesbian causes. For both, sex with other women is the essence of an erotic lifestyle.

BREAKING IN

Diana's body is so thin and linear that it's almost boyish. One can't help getting the feeling that her shape and the short cut of her hair are designed to announce her lesbianism to the world. She is five-foot-nine, with brown hair. Her high cheekbones give her brown eyes a permanently questioning look, as though everything she sees comes as a surprise. She is in her late twenties but says that, based on when she became sexually mature, she's a lot younger than that.

It's a miracle I have any erotic lifestyle at all. I had a strict religious upbringing and received my entire education in parochial schools. The only sex education I had in high school was designed to brainwash me into believing that any sex outside of marriage was so sinful that it would damn me to the eternal flames. When other girls I knew were experimenting with young men in the backseats of cars, I was praying for help in remaining pure.

The first time I was kissed by a boy was on my twelfth birthday. It was supposed to be a friendly birthday kiss, but when he tried to put his tongue in my mouth, I gagged. I was so horrified, I didn't let a boy kiss me again until I was in my senior year of high school. That too was a disappointment. I felt nothing but guilt and remorse. The kiss wasn't even worth it.

I went to a college that actually made all students sign a pledge that they would refrain from sexual activity until they were married. I took it quite seriously when I made the vow, but my hormones were those of any normal female approaching adulthood. So I dated a bit and occasionally let one of my dates feel my breasts. Once a boy even got to put his hand under my skirt and touch me between the legs. I didn't find it exciting or arousing or even pleasant. It wasn't until after I graduated that I actually did have sexual intercourse. It happened with two different men, but both times I had the same negative feelings. I hated it. I thought that was because of the guilt I was experiencing. I didn't learn the real reason until after I went to work at my present job.

I'm a software engineer, with a company located in the heart of the Silicon Valley in northern California. I won't mention which one. Like many such companies, it was founded by a couple of guys in their twenties who got their start in a garage somewhere. Now it's publicly traded and worth millions, but the founders managed to retain their youthful, informal style of management. All the employees are permitted to dress any way they want. Everyone is on a first-name basis with everyone else. Nobody has the title of "supervisor" or is regarded as a boss of any kind. The person who oversees my work is known simply as "Senior Software Engineer," the idea being that he mentors rather than supervises.

Glenn—that's his name—and I are very friendly, both at work and away from work. We have had many frank conversations. He started telling me about his sex life with his wife, and I felt quite comfortable telling him about mine, or the lack of same. When I explained how I thought my religious upbringing had ruined things for me, he just smiled and flashed an understanding look, as though he knew something about me that I didn't. It turned out that he did.

He told me that he limited his own sexual contacts to his wife Marlene, but that she had sex partners besides him. I was startled by this and began to ask him about it. "You mean she goes with other men?" I stammered.

He laughed. "No," he said. "I'll admit, I wouldn't tolerate that. She's bi and sometimes feels a need to be with another woman. I really don't mind it. In fact, they occasionally let me watch, and I find that very exciting."

That shocked me even more. I had heard of women who have sex with other women, but the people I knew always referred to them by nasty names that I don't even like to repeat. It seemed so unnatural. At the same time, though, the thought lodged in my mind and titillated me in a funny kind of way. I wanted to ask Glenn more about it but was too embarrassed. So I was glad when something came up to interrupt our conversation.

About a week later, Glenn asked if I'd like to have a drink with him after work. He said that Marlene might be joining us at the cocktail lounge. I had met her at a few company parties and thought she was a very nice person, so I gladly accepted. It wasn't until afterwards that I remembered what he had told me about her and wondered how I was going to be able to make idle conversation with her now that I knew of her strange sexual tastes.

After Glenn had a drink and I had two, his wife showed up. I joined her for another, while Glenn continued nursing his. Conversation was awkward at first, but after two more drinks, I found myself quite comfortable with her. At some point, Marlene said she wanted a cigarette, and I did too. The bar was a nonsmoking establishment—I think all California bars have to be—so we went outside.

After a few moments of silence, Marlene said, "Glenn tells me you don't have much of a sex life. Is that so?"

Maybe if I hadn't been drinking, I would have been a little put out by Glenn's sharing my secrets with his wife. At that moment, it seemed natural, though, so I just said, "I'm afraid it is."

"Have you ever tried another woman?" she asked. When I just shook my head in embarrassed silence, she said, "Well, maybe you should." With that, she reached out and tweaked my nipple with her fingers. It happened so fast, I had no chance to react. We finished our smokes and went back inside.

I knew I was in no condition to drive, so I was relieved when Glenn, who was still working on his first drink, offered to take me home. He said he'd bring me back for my car the next day. The three of us went out to Glenn's car and he opened a back door for me. I got in and was a little surprised to see Marlene getting in beside me. "Don't want to leave you all alone back here," she explained as Glenn started the engine and drove off.

Suddenly, I felt Marlene put a hand on my leg and move it slowly up my thigh. My first instinct was to slap away the intruding hand, but a combination of intoxication and some strange sort of curiosity stopped me. A moment later, her hand was under my skirt. Looking me right in the eye, she whispered, "Unbutton your top." Like a computer following the program, I did as she said, my numb fingers twisting at the buttons of my blouse until it was wide open and my bra was showing. With her free hand, she pulled the material down until my nipples were exposed. "Nice," she murmured.

I was surprised to feel my nipples hardening. Usually, they only reacted that way when desperation drove me to masturbate. I always tried to get that nasty operation over as quickly as possible. This, though, was exquisite. Her fingers were gently touching and petting my nipples while she cooed soft sounds. I found it quite exciting.

I was astounded when she leaned toward me and pressed her lips to mine in a passionate kiss. I remembered the boy who stuck his tongue in my mouth at my birthday party and was prepared to gag. But when her tongue played over my teeth and gums, I found the sensation arousing. I think I was more excited sexually at that moment than I had ever been before in my life. I could see Glenn watching in the mirror and didn't feel the least bit bothered by it.

As Marlene kissed me, her hand moved up my skirt. I held my breath, not even willing to imagine what she would do next. I felt her hooking her finger through the crotch of my very damp panties, tugging and pulling until they began sliding down. I'm sure I lifted myself slightly off the seat to assist her in removing them. When she had them off, she reached over the front seat and handed them to her husband, saying "What do you think?" He sniffed them and smiled. I could hear the engine roar as he stepped down on the accelerator in an obvious hurry to get somewhere.

When the car came to a stop a few minutes later, I realized we were not in front of my apartment as I had expected, but in the driveway of a nice suburban home. "You two will be more comfortable inside," Glenn said. He opened the door for me to get out.

I was flustered and nervous, but I was so hot that I think I would have followed Marlene straight into hell if she cared to lead me in that direction. She took my hand and led me into the bedroom, where she turned on a dim lamp. My blouse was still wide open, but I had pulled the bra back up over my breasts. As I sat on the edge of the bed, I was painfully conscious of the fact that I had no panties on. I stared dumbly at Marlene as she quickly shed her clothes.

After her dress fell to the floor, she stood in a pink bra and matching pink panties. They didn't cover much. I could see her dark nipples through the material, and little tendrils of pubic hair showed around the leg bands of the tiny undies. I was astonished to find myself becoming aroused at the sight of her. Looking at the two naked men I had seen never had any effect on me at all.

Shucking the undergarments, she let me see her fully nude, turning slowly in place so I would miss nothing. Then, stepping up to where I sat dumbfounded, she took my head in her hands and pressed her breasts against my face. I felt one erect nipple touching my lips. Without any thought, I began sucking on it. I felt goose bumps forming all over me and my face reddening with heat as I heard her draw her breath in sharply at the contact of my mouth with her sensitive nipple.

My head whirled when her hands began relieving me of my clothes. Soon I was as naked as she, without any opportunity to be embarrassed about it. For some strange reason, this felt right. I was being seduced by a woman and finding sexual excitement for the first time ever. I didn't stop to think about it. I just let my inner programming take over.

I still don't know how I got there, but a moment later I was lying on my back, fully nude, with Marlene, also nude, lying beside me on the bed. Her hands were everywhere, stroking my breasts, gently rubbing my belly, spreading the lips of my pussy, touching my clit. Wherever her fingers strayed, she left a trail of fire that consumed me with its heat. I didn't know what to do, so I just lay there letting it happen.

Now she was running her fingers up and down my slit, picking up bits of my own moisture to spread over my clit and pussy lips. Before I knew it, her head was buried in my groin. I could feel her hot breath on my opening. Then I felt her lips closing softly around the button of my clit. I had touched it many times to bring myself relief, but she seemed to know ways of giving me something new and different. Not just a climb toward rapid relief, but pleasure that made me want it to last for as long as possible.

So this is why people like sex. I had no idea anything could feel this wonderful. I wanted to make her feel as good as I did. She seemed to sense that and moved her body so that her knees were on either side of my head, her face still pressed against my pussy. I could see her hair-fringed opening looming above me. I could smell the fragrance of it. God, how I wanted to taste it.

Lifting my head slightly, I brought my mouth against her opening. I had no idea what I was doing, but that didn't stop me. I began to lick and lap and roll my tongue over and around her sex, savoring the flavors of a woman's pussy for the first time. It's a flavor I've learned to love, but that night it was a revelation, a discovery, a gift from heaven. The alcohol I had drunk earlier was nothing compared to the intoxicant I was now sucking up hungrily.

Marlene's fingers were working me open so that her tongue could plunge inside me, fucking me like a man's penis never could. I tried to imitate her movements and do the same to her. The soft moans I heard coming from her throat made me feel powerful. I was actually giving her pleasure, something I never gave to a partner before.

I could taste a change in the flavors of her juices and knew instinctively that she was going to have an orgasm. I wanted her to, more than anything. I wanted to make her come. As soon as I realized that, I felt my own climax arriving. I was confused, uncertain. Should I let it go? Should I allow myself to come in her mouth? Should I give her a warning?

Before I could focus enough to even try to answer those questions, I felt all my emotions gushing through my vagina. I sobbed as the first rush of orgasm hit me. I howled when it resounded from the walls of my pussy to start a second wave. I began to scream when it flowed fully in, around, through, and throughout me. A moment later, Marlene's hips started to buck as she too began the staccato cries of pleasure.

It went on for millennia, before the intensity of the sensations started to subside. When the orgasm was finished, I felt totally drained, weak, exhausted, but filled with a new excitement. Fulfillment was possible for me. I had an orgasm with a woman and I didn't even feel guilty about it. It was right. It was righteous.

That was my coming-out party. From that moment on, I knew why I had never been able to find satisfaction with a male partner. I'm a lesbian. Nothing in my former life had prepared me for that realization, but once Marlene's mouth brought me to orgasm, I had no problem accepting it. I'm a lesbian, and it's wonderful. I love being a lesbian. I love the feelings I get when I'm in the arms of another woman.

It didn't take me long to learn about lesbian culture: where to find partners, how to behave in the straight world and in the lesbian world, how to be happy with who I am. I have had many female lovers since then.

One of the pleasures I've discovered is the joy that comes from helping another latent lesbian discover who she is. Most of the lesbians I know enjoy being the first to introduce a formerly straight woman—or one who believed she was straight—into the satisfaction that comes from woman-to-woman sex. Most are only too glad to fulfill that function, to provide that entry for a straight woman into our world. Sometimes they can't, though, because of a family relationship they have with the person they want to bring in. Maybe "break in" would be a better way to put it.

So I've let the word get around that I'm available to break in newcomers to the lesbian life. I've always been grateful to Marlene for helping me find out who I really am. Now I enjoy playing that same role for other women. It has become the basis for my erotic lifestyle. I don't think a month goes by without my having the opportunity to enjoy one or two new disenchanted straights. More important, I manage to give them the opportunity to fulfill themselves sexually, often for the first time.

SELF-EXAMINATION

Umeko is too small to be called petite. Tiny would be a better charac-terization. She's not much more than five feet tall, with narrow shoulders and a very slender, although curvy, figure. Her shoulder-length hair is glossy black, and her almond-shaped Asian eyes match its color. Her small hands are very expressive, moving rapidly to emphasize whatever she is saying. She wouldn't tell us her age, except to say that she's under thirty.

I've always known I was a lesbian. I can't tell you how. I just knew it. I never had sexual contact with a male and never intend to. I'm just not interested. Now, women? That's another matter altogether. I've had between ten and fifteen female sex partners in my life. At the moment, I have a steady partner. Between her and my job, I get all the sex I need.

Like all the other partners I've had, she shares my feelings about the sight of the female body. You'd be surprised at how many women, even lesbians, think the female body is unattractive. It has to do with the way they were indoctrinated by society, made to feel inferior. Lots of women have allowed Hugh Hefner and the boys to tell them what beauty is. So they find fat disgusting, and they find sagging tissue horrible, and they regard small bosoms as pathetic, and they think there is some kind of paradise that comes with breast implants.

I, on the other hand, love the sight of the naked female body, no matter what shape it's in. When I was in high school, I discovered the pleasures of the locker room. I was what every straight male dreams of being—an unnoticed observer in a women's changing room. I'd look forward to gym class all day long. Then, as my classmates and I got in and out of our outfits, I'd feast my eyes on all the naked girls. A sea of developing breasts and bottoms and vulvas as far as my eye could see. It was even more exciting knowing they could see me.

The only problem was that I had to be casual about looking at them. And even though I might be fully naked in their midst, I could never be sure anyone was looking at me. So, as exciting as it was, in some ways it was frustrating, too.

In college, it was the same. I majored in physical education, because I love sports and body culture, but also because it gave me more opportunities to see and be seen in the locker room. By then, of course, we were all older, so the sights were much more interesting. Most of the women I knew in school were quite aware of my sexual affinities, so I had to be even more circumspect in my watching. It's funny, if they didn't know I was being sexually turned on by the sight of them, they probably would have had no hesitation in stripping and walking around naked in front of me. Knowing it, though, inhibited them. So I tried not to make a big deal out of seeing them.

After college, I joined athletic clubs just for the locker room experiences. There, too, I had to behave myself so I wouldn't frighten the women. It's fun to sneak peeks, but I really prefer an intense study. Even though I'm physically faithful to whatever partner I happen to have at the moment, I love to look at other women. Most of my partners have felt the same way.

A few years ago, I began to get active in lesbian organizations. One was an alternative women's health center, a clinic that specializes in the problems of homosexual women. At first, I just went there one evening a week to stuff envelopes and make phone calls attempting to raise money. Once while I was there, I saw a sign advertising a self-examination workshop. I don't like going to doctors, especially since the medical establishment seems to be run by men. But I know the importance of detecting disease early, so I signed up for the workshop.

There were four attendees, including me, and one instructor, who, like the rest of us, was a lesbian. She explained the importance of early detection and of monthly self-examination and then proceeded to demonstrate on herself. Oh, I was in paradise. Not only did she expose her breasts and vulva, but we were invited to look. We were supposed to watch closely, to find out how to do the self-exam. Then each of us took a turn trying it while everyone else watched and the instructor critiqued. It was wonderful. When the instructor told us she was leaving to take a job in another state, I made a career decision on the spot.

The very next day, I told the supervisor of the health center that I wanted to become a self-examination instructor. She said she was very glad to hear it because it's hard to find good instructors. When she told me that the job didn't pay very much and asked me why I wanted it, I said that I thought of self-examination as a tool for self-discovery and empowerment. It helps women not only to achieve better health, but to know what we have always been told we were not supposed to know. It helps us to assert ownership over our own bodies. I really do believe all that, but I said it mainly because I knew it was what she wanted to hear.

I was hired and began my training a few days later with the woman who had been the instructor at the workshop I attended. It was great to be one-on-one with her, looking at her breasts and vagina and having her look at mine. The training went on for three days. Each evening when I went home, I'd be so turned on that I'd devour the woman I was living with.

A week later, I began running the workshops myself, usually for three or four women at a time. Most of our clients are lesbians, but not all of them. I conduct the workshop in two sessions, one for breast examination and one for vaginal examination. I arranged to have several full-length mirrors installed on the walls of the room we use.

I usually spend the first half hour getting acquainted. We all introduce ourselves using first names only and talk a little about our background. I explain why the American Cancer Society recommends self-examination once a month for all women over the age of twenty and I talk about what self-examination is. Even though we all grow up changing our clothes together in communal situations, most women are a little inhibited about undressing in front of other women in small groups. So I want to be sure everyone is fully relaxed before we actually get to work.

Finally, when I feel that the time is right, I say that the most important step we will take is to become comfortable with the idea of examining ourselves visually and with our hands. As I speak, I casually unbutton my shirt. I don't usually need or care to wear a bra, but I am always sure to have one on for the workshops, so the women who are wearing them will feel better about being seen in and out of them. I lay my shirt over a chair and continue speaking, moving around in my bra for a few minutes before reaching back to unsnap it. I act as though I'm having trouble and finally ask one of the women present to help me. By now, it seems natural for us all to be undressing together and assisting each other.

As soon as the bra is off, I invite the rest of the women to do the same. Typically, some are braless. Those wearing bras frequently end up helping each other out of them. Occasionally someone will hesitate, but most are ready to fall right in with the program. Those who are hesitant always come around when everyone else is nude from the waist up. It's funny, being the only one dressed can be just as embarrassing as being the only one undressed might be.

When we're all topless, I demonstrate how to stand in front of the mirror and visually examine both breasts for any change in the shape or contour. I clasp my hands behind my head and press forward. This flexes the muscles of the chest and raises the breasts for inspection. Then, placing my hands firmly on my hips, I lean slightly forward, looking for any dimpling, puckering, nipple changes, or spontaneous nipple discharge. It's really quite simple.

After I've shown them what to do, I have each of them try it while the rest of us watch and I give pointers. Unfortunately, for many women, it's the first time they've actually spent time studying their own breasts without comparing themselves to centerfold models. I'm telling you that watching them flexing their pectoral muscles and staring at their breasts is a tremendous turn-on for me. I wouldn't tell them because of that inhibition thing I mentioned earlier. Self-examination is no time for inhibitions.

I explain that the shower is a good place for manual breast self-exam, because soapy fingers slide easily over the skin, permitting you to feel anything unusual. During the workshop, I give each woman a small bottle of baby oil for lubricating her fingers. After oiling my own, I raise one hand above and behind my head and use the opposite hand to feel my breasts. With the flat pads of the middle three fingers, I feel for swollen or lumpy areas. I move my fingers in small circles to feel the tissue beneath them, sliding from one area of the breast to the next. Beginning at the outside border, I work my way around the breast and squeeze each nipple, looking for discharge. Finally, I check the areas under the collarbones and arms.

I'm diligent about my own self-exam and about teaching the other women what to do. But that doesn't stop me from getting excited when they're watching me and even more excited when I watch each of them. My nipples get very hard. That's natural with all the breast touching going on, so nobody thinks anything of it. I just love watching the other women's nipples becoming erect, too. Especially when I see it happen while they're watching me, even before they begin examining themselves.

Next, I teach them how to do the self-examination while lying down. We provide thin mattresses on the floor for that purpose. I flatten my right breast by placing a pillow under my right shoulder and my right arm behind my head. I feel for lumps by rubbing in small, dime-sized circles. They kneel around my mattress watching me intently, which heightens my excitement. Then each of them does the same, while we all gather around her. I never touch any of the women, because that would clearly be unethical. I do think, however, that as long as I'm doing a good job teaching them these important techniques, there's no harm in my letting it affect me sexually, especially since I have no control over my body's responses.

In the next session, I teach them the techniques of vulvar and vaginal self-examination. Most women don't even realize there's a difference between the vulva and vagina. The vulva is the external part of the genital organs. For lesbians, it's that very special area where most of our sexual contact takes place. The vagina is internal, the canal leading from the vulva to the cervix, which is the entrance to the womb. It can't be seen without the aid of a special instrument called a speculum.

We begin with the vulva. Most lesbians have looked closely at their partners' vulvas, but it's surprising how few ever really look at their own. By this time, the women in the workshop are accustomed to being partially nude with each other. So as soon as the second session begins, I take off my pants and panties and invite all of them to do the same. I like to keep my bush full and natural and I like to feel them looking at it while I speak.

Finally, I turn my mattress so that I can lie on it with my feet pointed at the mirror. I bend my knees and put my feet flat against the mattress, spreading my legs as far as I comfortably can. Even though most lesbians are more conversant with a woman's body than straight women tend to be, I like to make sure we're all on the same page. So I name each part as I show them what to look for.

First, the mons pubis, that area above the vulva where the pubic hair is located. I can practically feel their eyes on me as I spread the curls to check visually for bumps, warts, ulcers, or changes in skin color and as I run my fingers over the sensitive skin to feel for bumps below the surface. Next, the clitoris and area around it. By this time, I'm usually so aroused that mine is sticking out and smiling at them. I love to see them smile back. Most women just refer to the lips of their vulva as labia, but I show them the difference between the labia minora, which are the smaller folds of skin just to the right and left of the opening, and the labia majora, which are the larger folds of skin just outside the labia minora.

As I tell them this, I show them by holding my own vulva wide open with my thumb and fingers. Then raising my hips, I exhibit the perineum, that strip between the vulva and the anus. Finally, the area surrounding the anal opening. At each step, I show them what to look for and demonstrate how to examine by feel. It actually makes me quite hot to run my fingers over my vulva and anus while they are watching, and I know that my wetness is showing, which makes it even more exciting.

Each of the women takes a turn in front of the mirror, exposing and examining her own vulva and anus. The rest of us watch. It's a wonderful feeling for me to be able to look closely at another woman's genitals without having to sneak a peek. Not only do I get to stare openly, my job even requires me to make comments. They can all see my naked vulva, but it's a good thing they can't see that erogenous zone inside my head.

When every woman in the class has shown her vulva to me and the rest of the group while visually and manually inspecting it herself, it's time for me to demonstrate the technique for self-examination of the vagina. For this, I distribute hand mirrors, flashlights, tubes of water-based lubricant, and sterile plastic speculums. A speculum is a medical instrument used for spreading the vulva to permit examination of the vaginal canal.

Lying back with my knees up and apart, I spread a bit of lubricant over my labia minora and slip the tips of my fingers inside to put some there, too. This is necessary to facilitate comfortable insertion of the speculum, but with the other women watching I get the same feeling from it as when I'm finger-fucking myself for my partner to see as sexual foreplay. I have to do my best to hide the waves of pleasure I feel washing over my entire body.

Once I'm properly lubricated, I insert the speculum in the closed position, twisting it a little as it goes in. Then I pull the handle toward me until I feel it open within my vagina. I prop the hand mirror up on the mattress and position it until I can see inside. Then, shining the flashlight into the mirror, I move the speculum until I can see the cervix and vaginal walls in the mirror. At this point, the women gather around and stare either at the hand mirror or directly into my open vulva. The feeling I get from their attention is exquisite.

I talk about the color of the cervix and ask them to look for vaginal secretions. I explain the abnormalities that we are trying to discover and illustrate the various internal parts that should be examined as closely as possible. Then I have each of the women lie on the mattress and repeat the procedure on themselves. Oh, I really love that part. Sometimes, I get down on my knees between her legs and peer intently into her vagina. This gets me so hot that I often fear my juices will run down my legs. Fortunately, that hasn't happened.

After all have shown the ability to perform a proper self-exam, I return to the mattress and demonstrate proper use of a rubber dental dam, or female condom, for safe sex. In a way, this is the best part of the experience for me, because now while they're all looking at my vulva, I'm actually talking about oral sex. I refer to the parts that are most likely to be licked and played with and I show how to protect them with the rubber sheet. I also put on latex finger condoms, available in most sex shops, and demonstrate how important it is to use them during manual stimulation. This is great, because it gives me an opportunity to stroke my clit and finger-fuck myself as a legitimate part of the lecture.

There are times when it takes all the strength I've got to keep from having an orgasm. Once, I actually did let go and came while three or four women were watching. While it was taking place, I found it incredibly exciting. But afterwards, even though the ladies in the group were very understanding about it, I was so embarrassed I resolved never to let it happen again.

Now I fight like hell to hold back the climax. I can tell you this, though. When I get home that evening, my partner can always tell it was a workshop day. I tend to be so stimulated that I come the second she touches me. Then I come again and again all night long.

I love my work. I really feel I'm doing something important. In addition to helping the women who come to my classes maintain their good health, I feel I'm empowering them. I'm giving them the ability to regain control over their own bodies, to take them back from the male medical establishment that has dominated them for so long. To be honest, though, I can't deny that the erotic aspects of my work are what I like best. They merge my occupation and my private life into a wonderfully erotic lifestyle.

9

TAKE MY HUSBAND, PLEASE!

ACCORDING TO SOME OF THE MASS MEDIA, MATE swapping was a common suburban pastime throughout the United States during the late 1960s and early '70s. The chances are that this was not true. Although it occurred, it was not nearly as widespread as those who wrote about it wanted the rest of us to believe. In reality, there have always been marriages in which the partners felt completely at ease sharing each other with outsiders, but these have been the exception rather than the rule.

The stories in this chapter demonstrate that the swinging and mate-swapping phenomena continue to exist. Those who engage in such activities on a regular basis refer to their recreation simply as "the lifestyle." Annual "lifestyle" conventions held in various states and countries are living proof that swinging is still something that goes on throughout the Western world.

Further evidence can be found in the experiences of Anthony and of Hilary. For Anthony and his mate, weekly attendance at gatherings of an organized club where group sex and partner exchange is the norm began as a search for complete sexual fulfillment. For Hilary and her husband, discreet mate-swapping provided a way of climbing the corporate ladder. Anthony's initial participation was willing and open.

Hilary's was angry and done in a spirit of revenge. In the long run, both found an erotic lifestyle that brings them pleasure and satisfaction.

SWING CLUB

Anthony is forty-two years old and prides himself on being a great lover and worshiper of women. He owns a beauty salon in a very prestigious neighborhood and is groomed in keeping with the image his salon projects. His charm and good looks put a person at ease immediately upon meeting him. He is trim and lean, standing just under six feet tall. His dark brown eyes seem to glow as he checks us over while leading us into the office at the rear of the salon. His white teeth are straight and bright enough to be used as an advertisement for a dental office. He is dressed meticulously in an obviously expensive designer shirt and trousers. The gold diamond ring he wears on his ring finger combines with his diamond-studded Rolex watch to announce his success. His hands move quickly while he speaks, as though wielding a pair of scissors.

I got married four years ago at the ripe old age of thirty-eight. Nobody I know ever thought I'd tie the knot, because I always liked going from woman to woman. I'm a great believer that men and women need lots of sexual variety. For the average couple, monogamy is all there is. In my dictionary, that's another word for "death." Lucky for me that I found a woman who agrees 100 percent with me. My wife, Gabey, and me, well, we're different.

Before I get to talking about our lifestyle, I need to fill you in on some background from before we were married. From the time I was old enough to go out with girls, I dated constantly. I think I've had every kind of sexual experience a person should have. I certainly had every kind of experience I wanted to have, which means every kind I could think of having.

I always knew that my sexual appetite was way above normal. When I was in my twenties, most of my male friends seemed pretty satisfied with the sex they were getting. Some were single. Some were married. Some of the married boys fooled around a little on the side. But sexually they were all more or less content. I never was.

I knew lots of different ladies who were willing and eager to have sex. Some of them had insatiable appetites like mine. But still I wasn't satisfied. I could fuck a woman for hours, doing every possible sexual act we could think of, but I just wasn't satisfied. The minute I left her, I'd be seeking another. I always felt a strong sexual urge. I found sexual turn-ons everywhere I went and with everything I did.

I was always on the sexual prowl, for something erotically interesting. I always managed to find it. In supermarkets, I'd try to spot women with low-cut tops, so I could sneak a peek at their cleavage. Driving at night, I'd be looking for windows with the shades open, in case I could be lucky enough to see a woman undressing. At the beach I'd be searching for women wearing tiny bikinis, in hopes of seeing a little tuft of pussy hair sticking out of the legband. I might have just finished fucking a new woman; I might have had a whole series of explosive orgasms; still I'd get a hard-on at the sight of another woman's exposed flesh. That's the unquenchable thirst I was talking about. I was getting all the sex a man could dream of and still I was frustrated.

I kept lists of potential sex partners, women I had been developing. The ones I had fucked or knew without a doubt that I could fuck were on my active list, the "A" list. The rest were on the "B" list, my waiting list. In spite of that abundance of sexual partners, I used to go barhopping occasionally just for the thrill of the hunt. That's what got this whole thing I'm going to tell you about started.

I met a lady at a bar. Let's call her Marianne. We had a few drinks and before long we were fucking like mad dogs in her loft apartment.

I saw her a few times after that. After a couple of dates, she told me an interesting story.

A girlfriend of hers had gone to a swing party with her fiancé. The party was at an isolated house out in the farm country beyond the limits of this city. They had to pay an admission charge to get in. The place was full of couples who were freely exchanging mates. She told me her girlfriend was curious enough to go, but when they got there, she and her fiancé were so embarrassed that they just couldn't stay. I had the definite impression that she was telling me this because she was curious and wanted to go there. For that matter, I was too. This would be a new experience for me. Something I had not yet tried. I told her to get the details from her friend, and we made a date to drive out there and check it out.

The house had a large living room with several couches and chairs. There were people sitting around talking and getting acquainted. There was also a kitchen filled with people who were eating and drinking. Some of the people were dressed, while others walked around naked. The person who admitted us told us that there were several bedrooms upstairs where people went to have sex. Each bedroom door had a sign that read OCCUPIED on one side and UNOCCU-PIED on the other. If the side showing said UNOCCUPIED, it meant the room was empty or whoever was in it wanted other people to come in and join them.

I was curious to check out the bedrooms upstairs, but Marianne wasn't ready for that. After a while, she started up a conversation with another couple, and I excused myself, telling them I'd be back momentarily. Moving quickly upstairs, I accidentally opened the door to one of the bedrooms that had an OCCUPIED sign on it. Lying on the bed were two women and one guy. One of the women was lying on her back, her legs spread wide, while the other woman was eating her pussy. The guy was behind that one on his knees, pumping her with his cock. They were so occupied that they never knew the door had opened. I closed it quietly and moved on.

The next room had an UNOCCUPIED sign on it, and I slowly

opened it. There were six naked people there. Three women and three men were twisted into a pretzel, each one eating another and all so engrossed in their sexual pleasures that they never knew that I was observing them.

When I opened the next UNOCCUPIED door, there were one woman and one man just about to get it together. The woman was beautiful. The utter sight of her naked body made me feel short of breath. She was built like a brick shithouse, with tits the size of boulders and a body that was voluptuous, sensuous, and seemed to be calling out, *Fuck me.* I couldn't tear my eyes away from her. "Hi," she said when she saw me. "Why don't you come in and join us?"

The guy she was with I wouldn't recognize if I bumped right into him, because all I saw was her. I was so mesmerized by her good looks and magnificent body that I just stared. Her red hair hung loose and flowed down way past her shoulders. Her black saucer eyes intoxicated me. I just wanted to grab her and swallow her up.

The minute I laid eyes on her I felt some kind of bond. It wasn't a mere attraction. It was something more, something so much more. I couldn't understand then what I really was feeling. All I knew was that I never before had this kind of desire. She walked over to where I was standing and held her hand out, beckoning me to come in. The only thing I was sure of was that I wanted her. "Come and join us," she murmured again. The closer she got to me the more tortured I felt. Oh, how I wanted her. I was about to enter the room, when I heard Marianne calling my name.

"I thought you might be up here," she said as she approached the open door. She stopped in her tracks when she saw the beautiful woman who stood stark naked in the doorway. I could see her eyes moving up and down as she measured and appraised the redhead.

"Come on in," the woman said again, gesturing to both of us. "The more the merrier."

I looked at my date, my eyes silently asking if she was willing to make it a foursome. At first she just stood frozen in her tracks, obviously considering it but not quite knowing what to say or do. I could see an expression of indecision on her face. There was a holding of collective breath as we all waited to see what her reaction would be. Then the indecisive look turned to one of distaste. "I want to go home, Anthony," she demanded. "Right now. I don't feel comfortable being here and I want to leave."

The naked beauty walked toward her and in a soft, gentle voice introduced herself as Gabey. Trying to calm her down, Gabey suggested a cocktail or a glass of wine, but Marianne refused. Gabey told her that when she first came to this house she too felt uncomfortable, but that in no time at all she felt right at home.

Her gentleman friend was sitting at the edge of the bed and he added, "We won't bite you. We only want to fuck you." He chuckled as he said it, but it had the opposite effect of what he was expecting.

Marianne looked at me and said curtly, "I'm ready to leave. I want you to drive me home."

Maybe I could have patched things up with her, but I wasn't sure I wanted to. I looked at Gabey and her friend and shrugged. What could I do? I wanted to stay, but we had come in my car and it was my responsibility to drive my date home as she demanded. "I'd better leave," I said in a low voice, addressing Gabey. "I can't tell you how disappointed I am because I sure wanted to get to know you better." I eyed her huge tits as I spoke to be sure she got my meaning.

"Me too," she said with a seductive smile.

I couldn't help myself. "Will you give me your phone number so I can call you sometime?" I knew that by coming on to another woman in Marianne's presence, I was being rude to her, but I couldn't let this beauty slip away from me.

"Absolutely," Gabey responded. Reaching into a handbag that was on a chair next to the bed, she handed me a business card. "Call me at work," she said.

As far as Marianne was concerned, that was the last straw. She turned on her heel and practically ran from the room. I followed her to the car and drove her home. All during the ride, neither of us said a word. She was angry at me, and I was angry at her for frustrating my desires. Needless to say we never saw each other again.

I called Gabey the following Monday, and we arranged to go back as a couple to that house in the boonies. That whole week kept me all excited. The anticipation of seeing Gabey again almost made me forget the other benefits of going to a swing club. I was in a constant state of arousal. I felt like a teenager. I just couldn't get this new woman out of my mind.

We drove out to the swing house together, and conversation flowed real easy. She turned out to be every bit as charming as she was beautiful. She told me a lot about herself. She was two years younger than I, and from what she said, her sexual appetite was a lot like mine. She told me she had been coming to this swing club for a couple of years. Before that, she said, she had never felt completely satisfied. The club gave her the variety she needed. She added that she found it very exciting to come there with a man knowing that he would end up fucking other women while she watched, and that he would watch her fucking other men. When she said this, the hairs stood up on the back of my neck.

We wasted no time once we arrived at the house. No shmoozing with other people, no eating or drinking. We just made a dash up the stairs and headed straight for one of the bedrooms. We left the UNOC-CUPIED sign out, but I was hoping to be alone with her for a while before sharing with others. As it turned out, that's just the way it happened. Inside the bedroom, Gabey was undressed within seconds. I quickly followed and we jumped onto the soft mattress together.

She was all over me at once, her hands touching my naked body, caressing and exploring my skin with her expert fingers. Her lips kissed me everywhere and found their way to my cock almost immediately. I could feel my big dick pulsating while it grew even bigger inside the warmth of her mouth. Gabey stroked my cock up and down, wetting it and then sucking in the juices with her tongue. She did it so expertly that I was soon groaning with bliss.

While she sucked me, I reached for two handfuls of her mountainous tits. They were soft and fleshy. My fingers petted the satiny tissue, exploring till they found her erect nipples. I felt my cock jerk the moment I touched them. They were unbelievably large, much bigger than any woman's I ever had. I wanted to caress and pet them all night long and never stop. Touching her nipples sent chills down my spine and brought me to new heights of excitement.

She was humming softly as she sucked my cock, the sound making all the membranes of her mouth and throat vibrate around me. Then, before I knew it, she let my cock slip from her mouth and she straddled me. Placing her hand on my hard-on, she aimed it in between her pussy lips and bore down hard and fast with her pelvis until my shaft was swallowed up deep inside her cavernous channel. With a satisfied smile, she looked down at me, our eyes meeting, and moved up and down in a steady fucking motion that drove me wild.

She leaned forward to drop her swaying boobs onto my lips. My mouth opened and I started to kiss and lick them all at the same time. The wetter her tits became, the harder her nipples got. My lips puckered around her large areolae while my tongue licked hard at her nipples. I felt like I was taking nourishment from her huge tits.

"Ooooooohh yes," she murmured. "I love that." Gabey was riding me hard, never losing the tempo of her rhythmic motion. My cock felt like it was swimming in a hot pool of swirling liquid. She reached back with one of her hands to caress my balls. Slowly her fingertips massaged my sack while her body kept up a steady fucking momentum.

I felt I was on the brink of an orgasm and I knew I had to stop because I didn't yet want to come. I rolled us both onto our sides and then rolled Gabey onto her back, pulling my cock from her pussy as abruptly as she had let it slip from her mouth a few minutes earlier. Kneeling at her feet, I placed my hands on the insides of her thighs, spreading them wide, and began to lick her sweet opening. She responded by pressing her pussy tight against my mouth and spreading her legs even wider.

I looked up at her and caught an expression on her face that completely delighted me. She looked as though she were in a trance, utterly lost in sexual meditation. Her body moved in time with my tongue, which was buried deep inside her now. I tasted every crease and crevice in the heated box of her womanhood. She groaned and rocked her hips each time I discovered a new hidden passageway.

I looked up to see her hands working her own tits, kneading them and holding them up and away from her body. She caught my eyes and smiled, her tongue elaborately licking her lips in imitation of my pussy lapping. Her immense nipples seemed to throb under her touch. They stood out straight and tall, like my cock, which was becoming longer and harder. I reached for her tits and put my hands on top of hers, helping her tweak the swollen nubs.

Gabey was purring like a kitten. "Anthony," she murmured. "I'm going to come." Her words excited me so much that I could actually hear my heart thumping. My tongue kept up a steady stroking of her interior until I heard a gasping scream issue from her lips and I knew I had brought her to completion.

She let me lick her for a long time, even after she came. What a woman. Most of the women I had known needed a break after coming, but not Gabey. She was a sex machine, just like I was. As I sucked her, she turned her body until we were in a sixty-nine position, with me on the bottom. She took my cock in her mouth while she pressed her pussy against mine. We were sucking each other simultaneously, our movements perfectly synchronized.

Gabey sucked hard on my cock while her hands stroked the insides of my thighs and tickled my balls. She seemed to know just the right places to touch me and just the right pressure to send my senses soaring. I drifted in and out of consciousness while her tongue and lips worked gently to bring me to the brink of my own exquisite orgasm. When it began, I grunted loud enough to wake the dead. I grunted again with each spurt that sprang from the tip of my cock. When my orgasm finally subsided, she just kept sucking.

We were still mouthing each other when we heard the door open. We both paused just for a moment to see who had come in. It was a couple. "Please don't stop," the pretty young woman said as she moved closer to the bed.

"Can we join the party?" her male partner asked.

Before I had a chance to answer, Gabey was all over them. She began helping the woman out of her clothes. "I'm Gabey and this is Anthony," she said breathlessly. Within seconds, the two strangers were naked and hopping into the bed beside us.

Gabey's hands immediately reached for the woman's pointy tits. At the same moment, the boyfriend began running his hands over Gabey's naked body. Not to be left out, I gently touched the young woman's pussy. It was already wet. With my other hand, I cupped her breast. Her titties were much smaller than Gabey's, and the change was exciting. I began moving my hand from Gabey's big tits to the other woman's smaller ones. What an exotic treat. The guy was kissing Gabey's pussy. As I watched, she lay on her back and spread her legs for him. He climbed on top of her at once.

I watched his body lower itself onto Gabey's as his hand guided his cock into her waiting pussy. As I saw her fucking this stranger, I knew I was in love. Each thrust of his cock into her made me love her more.

His girlfriend took the cue and rolled onto her back, spreading her legs wide and whisking me in. She was soaking wet inside, and her warm pussy swallowed me like a tasty treat. I watched Gabey being fucked while Gabey watched me fuck her partner's friend. We all moved up and down, each couple matching its rhythm to the other. The four of us fucked hard and furiously until the woman under me started to come. As soon as her male friend heard her cries of satisfaction, he too started to spurt, filling Gabey with his sperm.

When the fucking was over, the sucking began. Forming a circle, each of us feasted on someone else. Our new woman friend started to suck my cock. Gabey licked her pussy. The male stranger drove his tongue deep into Gabey's open pussy. All that left for me was to suck his cock, and I did. I could taste my Gabey's juices on him, and that made it exciting. It was the first time I had ever done it. There were a lot of firsts happening that night.

The room was filled with the sound of moaning and groaning and gurgling and sighing. Throwing all inhibitions aside, we touched and sucked every part of each other's bodies until we were able to orgasm again. After a while, the other woman held Gabey's pussy open for me and the other man stroked my cock and put it in her. Then he put his cock in her mouth while I fucked her. I think we both came in her at the same time.

I can't remember how many different people we had sex with that night. I do know it was the start of a truly satisfying sex life for me. We went back there every weekend, always finding new people to join us in group fucking and partner swapping. Gabey never got jealous when I started sex up with another woman, and I never got jealous when she got involved with other men. We loved watching each other, and we loved fucking other partners right next to each other in the same bed.

During the week, we had passionate sex with each other every night. Even that was satisfying. A deep love developed between us and we found ourselves spending more and more time together. I had never considered the thought of marriage before, but with Gabey it seemed like the natural thing for us to do. I can't even tell you who mentioned it first.

After we were married, we kept going back to the swing club for great weekend sex, until one day the fellow who ran the place told us that he was moving away. We felt terrible. The swap sessions had become so much a part of our lifestyle that we didn't know how we'd get along without them. The man made a proposition. He told us that he took in enough from couples who came there on the weekends to meet his mortgage payments and offered to sell us the place. He said he'd even finance it and agreed that if we ever had trouble making the payments, he'd be patient with us. We made the deal.

Now we are the operators of the weekend swing club. We still live in the city, of course. I still have the salon to run. Gabey has started her own graphic art business, which is really taking off. Our weekend parties are paying for the country house, and we think we might want to retire there in ten years or so. Meanwhile, it's the way we keep ourselves in swing partners and manage to maintain our very erotic lifestyle.

CORPORATE SUCCESS

Hilary is in her fifties and makes no attempt to hide it. If anything, the slight bluish rinse she gives her elegantly coifed silver hair emphasizes her age. She wears steel-rimmed glasses, behind which her blue eyes twinkle. Her face is wrinkle-free. She dresses in expensive but conservative clothing and carries herself like the wife of a corporate executive, which she is. She's about five-foot-seven and of medium build. Her soft curves underline her femininity.

My husband, Anson, started in an entry-level position with the company some thirty-odd years ago and is now a senior vice president. I like to think I had something to do with his rise to corporate success, although that was not what I originally had in mind. Revenge was uppermost in my thoughts on the night when it all started.

We were on our way to the home of Mr. Carmichael, Anson's new boss, shortly after his employment began. I was thrilled by the fact that we had been invited for a social visit by such an important company officer. Anson explained before we left that his career would depend to a great extent on how good an impression I made. He said I was being tested in the role of corporate wife. In the car, however, he set off a bomb.

"Hilary," he began in a hesitant tone. "When Mr. Carmichael asked me to bring you around for cocktails tonight, he hinted that he wanted to fuck you and wanted me to fuck his wife. I got the definite feeling that it's something expected of us if I'm going to succeed in this company. If you're willing, that is."

"If *I'm* willing," I answered, aghast. "If *I'm* willing? What about you? Is this something *you* want?"

I was even more shocked when he said, "Well, yes, it is. I mean, what the hell, you weren't a virgin when I met you. He could just as well be someone you fucked before we got married. What difference does it make before or after? I really think it will help my career. In the end it will benefit both of us financially."

I couldn't believe what I was hearing him say. It made me angry—so angry that I decided to get even. I'd fuck Mr. Carmichael, all right. I'd give him a better fuck than I ever gave Anson. Afterwards, I'd tell Anson how great it was. Then I'd tell him I was leaving him, the son of a bitch!

When we got to the Carmichaels' my mind was made up. As I shook Mr. Carmichael's hand, I squeezed it seductively and looked into his eyes with as much expression of sexual hunger as I could muster. He was rather handsome and dignified-looking, standing tall and erect, with broad shoulders and that look of good grooming that goes with money. I barely noticed Mrs. Carmichael. From what I did see of her, she was middle-aged and frumpy. I thought that would be poetic justice. I'd have a good time romping in bed with the boss, while my husband was stuck with Mrs. Ugly. Then I'd leave him so he'd be a loser all around.

I found myself nervous at the thought of being screwed by the good-looking executive. I was still angry, but a feeling of sexual excitement was starting to cover all other thoughts. I barely tasted the drink Mr. Carmichael gave me. At some point, I heard him saying something about some famous artist and asking whether I'd like to see the painting by him that they had recently purchased. Sensing that this was the moment, I said I would and let him lead me to his bedroom. I didn't care at all about what Anson would be doing with the dowdy wife. That was his problem.

As Mr. Carmichael closed the bedroom door behind us, he began to go through the motions of pointing to the painting that hung over the big canopied bed. I hardly listened. Instead, I reached behind me to unzip the cocktail dress I was wearing. He watched in silence as I stepped out of it and stood before him in my black lace underwear.

"Here," he said in a soft voice. "Let me help with that." He unsnapped my bra and freed my breasts.

It was clear that my willingness did not surprise him. I wondered what promise Anson had made and got angry all over again. As an

expression of my anger, I peeled off my pantyhose and the brief panties I wore underneath. Now I was naked and wishing my husband
could see me and eat his heart out.

Carmichael undressed without ceremony. Taking me by the hand,
he led me wordlessly to the bed and eased me down onto it. Then, to
my surprise, he began kissing me as though we were passionately in
love. At first, I found it offensive, as I found the whole episode. Little by little, though, his kisses began to warm me. When his hands
lightly brushed my breasts, I could feel my nipples stiffen. I was
becoming aroused.

He was quite a skillful lover. I remember thinking that his skill
probably came from fucking a lot of women, the wives of all his junior employees. Those thoughts began to fade, though, when his fingers found their way to my pussy. He touched it in a way Anson
never had. Within instants, I found myself getting dewy with excitement. Something in me wanted to hold on to my anger and carry it
with me throughout the ordeal, but I felt it fading against my will as
desire overpowered all my other emotions.

Involuntarily, my arms went around him as he pressed his body to
mine. A moment later, he was on top of me. I reached down for his
cock and found it swollen and pulsing with eagerness. I wrapped my
legs around his thighs to open for him and used the tips of my fingers
to guide him into me. This was no ordeal. It was an adventure.

As the executive began to pound me with his cock, I forgot all
about my husband and what he might be doing with Mrs.
Carmichael. For a fleeting instant, I feared the man would discharge
inside me and then withdraw, the way Anson sometimes did when he
fucked me. Carmichael kept moving steadily, though, altering his
tempo every few strokes. He pumped fast in and out of me, then
pushed forward and back very gradually, dragging out each movement until it seemed forever. Then he pumped fast again. Each vari-
ation increased the sensations.

It wasn't long before I felt an orgasm coming. There was no anger
at all anymore. Just sheer pleasure. It was incredible how this

stranger's technique had overwhelmed any emotional resistance I felt at first. Now I was on the edge of climax. Now I was tumbling over the edge. As the surges of ecstasy wended their way through my pussy, I began to whine. Then I sobbed. Finally, I began to scream. It was the best cum I had for as long as I could remember.

I shouted my satisfaction to the heavens, mildly aware that my partner was coming with me. His cock was swelling and relaxing inside me as hot gushes of cum shot from his dick against the opening of my womb. He grunted like a hungry savage, taking his pleasure with me as I took mine with him.

When it was over, we lay together in silence, and I thought again about the situation. I couldn't really be angry anymore. This had been too good. At first, I had resented Anson's using me as a commodity to be traded for career advancement. Now, though, I could hardly be resentful of his having given me such a wonderful sex experience. I even found myself hoping that he was having as good a time with his boss's wife as I had with his boss.

Eventually, the four of us met up again in the living room. We all had another cocktail, but we really did not have much to say to each other. So, in as polite a way as possible, Anson and I said we had to be going and left. The Carmichaels didn't make any effort to stop us.

In the car, Anson asked if everything had gone all right. I tried to subdue the excitement I was feeling. "Fine," I answered as casually as I could. "You?"

"Not too bad," he said. Then he chuckled. "Actually, the old girl was pretty good. I don't imagine that stodgy husband of hers gives her very much. It must have been a real drag for you to screw him?"

I felt a need to let him know that I had thoroughly enjoyed the experience, so I told him right out. "No, not a drag at all," I answered. "In fact, he gave me a damn good fucking."

Maybe I was hoping Anson would be somewhat jealous, although I didn't feel the least bit jealous of his time with the boss's wife. I wasn't really disappointed, though, when he said, "That's great. I'm really glad to hear it. Because I have a feeling that's what advancement in this company requires. How would you feel about doing the same sort of thing with some of the other execs?"

That was the beginning of our very exciting erotic lifestyle. We worked our way up through various levels of management, fucking our way to the top, you might say. Soon, it became a necessary part of our private sex life. We hardly ever made love without telling each other in detail about some of the things we had done on our swap outings.

It's interesting to think back on the sex partners we've had over the years. At first, they were always older than we were, because Anson was at a junior level and the swapping was with people above him, all of whom had been with the company longer. Then we found ourselves fucking people our own age who just happened to be higher up than Anson. After a while, we were swapping laterally, with people at the same level as Anson, but in different branches of management. Now that he has advanced to a senior position, we get our pick of the younger employees. God, I don't know what we'll do for fun when he retires.

10

NOT
EXACTLY BI

SOME BISEXUALS CLAIM TO HAVE TWICE AS MUCH FUN
as the rest of us because they have twice as many potential sex
partners. Maybe that's true. Since most sex has nothing to do with
procreation, perhaps there is no real reason to restrict carnal contact
to members of the opposite gender.

The stories in this chapter are about people who have sex with
members of both genders, so we can't call them heterosexual. They
are not really bisexual either, because same-sex encounters are the
only ones they truly enjoy. On the other hand, since they live what
appear to be conventional married lives, we cannot classify them as
homosexual.

As far as we know, no accurate statistics have been compiled on
people like them who are married but prefer sex with members of
their own gender. After all, if people who feel that way were able to
deal honestly with their sexuality, they probably would not have married in the first place or would not have stayed married after discovering the true nature of their desires. How, then, can they be
expected to deal honestly with sex-survey takers and researchers?

Benton always believed he was undersexed and found it hard to
understand why his friends seemed so obsessed with sexuality. Joyce

regarded sex as nothing more than a price she had to pay for her husband's generosity. It took erotic encounters with members of their own genders to show them that sex could be exciting and fulfilling. For his or her own reasons, however, each remains married, indulging this newfound erotic lifestyle only on rare occasions.

LINGERIE BOUTIQUE

Joyce has curly brown hair that just about covers the back of her neck. The short cut and style is flattering to her delicate face. Her doe eyes and brown skin are highlighted by prominent and angular cheekbones. Joyce's small-boned frame gives the appearance of petiteness, although she measures five feet five inches tall. She has a button nose that wrinkles up when she speaks in an expressive tone. She wears an expensive designer outfit that makes her stand out from the crowd, and she is draped in gold jewelry that catches the eye with its sparkle. Her birthday was just a few days ago, and she tells us with a simulated frown that she has turned a corner and no longer can say that she is in her twenties. The three of us are alone in her lingerie boutique when we interview her.

I am married and have been for the past four years. My husband, Saunder, is considerably older than I, but there are advantages to that. When I met Saunder, he was already well established financially, with a business that afforded us a comfortably affluent lifestyle. He owned a beautiful house that had been decorated by a famous interior designer and he drove a Mercedes sports car. Frankly, his possessions are probably what first attracted me to him. As a wedding gift, he bought me something I had always dreamed of having, a brand-new Porsche. It's been that way ever since. Whatever material item I want, I get.

My husband does a lot of traveling for his business, but I really don't miss him much when he's away. During the first year of our marriage, I just stayed home and enjoyed my newfound luxury. I had quit my job because I felt no need to work. Before meeting Saunder, I was employed by a lovely couple who owned a fashionable boutique. Besides the salary, which was decent, they gave me a big discount on any clothes I bought at their shop.

After a while, though, in spite of the fact that I no longer needed the money or the discounts, I began to miss working. Doing nothing was a bore, and I missed the interesting experiences I used to have at the boutique. When I worked there, I would help customers pick out things that I thought would complement their figures and then I would assist them in the dressing room. It was there that I discovered a side of me that I guess I had been hiding even from myself and never really dealt with.

When I would go with customers into the dressing room and they would only be covered in their bras and panties, I would feel a certain excitement. The sight of their almost nude bodies had a peculiar effect on me. At first, I didn't question it or attempt to understand it. I think it frightened me a little, so I tried to ignore it.

Occasionally that got difficult, though, like when women would come in who were not wearing a bra. When I went into the dressing room with them, they would stand there in front of the mirror with just their panties on. I couldn't help but scope them out from head to toe, and my eyes would always feast on their naked breasts. At first, I rationalized this by telling myself that there was nothing wrong with healthy curiosity about the way other women's bodies looked. After all, everyone likes to look at a woman with a beautiful tight shape. Why shouldn't I? But it puzzled me that those incidents would get me aroused sexually and keep me in that condition for the rest of the day.

It was even more intense when I actually made physical contact with a practically naked woman, when my hands would actually touch their bare skin. Then I found myself feeling something unsatiable.

I used to fantasize about fitting them for lingerie, making sure a bra fit properly, for example, so I could run my fingers over them. I even dreamed about having my own lingerie shop, where I would sell only top-end merchandise, the kind of garments that needed personal care in fitting and selection.

As the boredom of staying home began to weigh on me, I became moody and depressed. Those old daydreams began returning. I would sit in a big easy chair with my eyes closed and imagine an endless line of glamorous women coming into my store and asking me to help them with expensive underwear. I pictured the way they would look and even the way it would feel as I touched them while fitting their bras and other undergarments. Finally, I mentioned my unhappiness to my husband, although naturally I didn't say anything about those fantasies or thoughts of other women.

Saunder is such a nice guy. He would do anything for me. So when I told him that my days were feeling long and empty, he was real understanding and said he wanted to make everything all right. He asked me what he could do to make life better. When I told him I wanted to try my own business, he was perfectly all right with that, never mentioning the cost. He even helped me find a good location for the shop.

As far as money, he told me he had deep pockets and I was to spare no expense. "Do whatever you want and buy whatever is necessary," he instructed. He said he had great faith that I would be successful. He was extremely giving and denied me nothing. I was grateful for his generosity and patience, knowing all along, of course, that if my business didn't take off, the money he spent setting me up would at least give him a tax write-off.

We got a designer to plan the interior. As you can see, she did an excellent job. I especially love the dressing rooms with all walls mirrored. The customers like it, because they can examine the fit from all directions. I like it even more, because it allows me to have complete views of their bodies, front and back. I sometimes get to see their naked breasts, vaginas, and bare bottoms, all at the same time.

Right from the start, I loved being in business. It occupied my days and kept me from being bored. More importantly, it gave me the opportunity to nourish my newly discovered interest in women's bodies. Most of the lingerie I carry comes from France. Nothing but the best for my ladies. It tends to be very revealing and very luxurious and requires just the right fit. Women who spend that kind of money expect to be pampered. They want me to help them undress and assist them into the garments they are trying on. They want me to assure them that the size and style is right. I'm only too glad to oblige.

In the course of serving my clientele, I get to see them and touch them. It's especially exciting when a woman needs to be fitted for a bra. It gives me a chance to touch her breasts and sometimes even her nipples. I fasten the bra and then put my hand inside the cup to adjust the breast, pulling each breast gently into position to be sure the cups are properly filled. I love the feel of their nipples against my hand. When they stir at my touch, I love it even more.

At first, the looking and touching kept me in a constant state of arousal. The problem was it never really got satisfied. My husband and I had occasional sex whenever he wanted it, which is not often. Sex just is not one of his priorities, maybe because he's older and absorbed with other things. When we do make love, it's never anything great. I always pretend to be overjoyed with his abilities as a lover. I owe him that. But I never feel sexually fulfilled by him. Actually, I don't think I ever felt sexually fulfilled by any man.

Instead, I lived in daydreams of sex with other women. More and more, my fantasies revolved around women who came into my shop. I found it funny to realize that I had never conjured the thought of sex with another man. Then one day in the store, my life took a turn that changed me forever.

It was the middle of the week. Soon after I opened the store, a lovely woman came in. I had never seen her before. We started to talk. She said she was new in the area and glad to discover a store like mine. Talking with her came easy. I felt she and I could become friends. I found myself attracted to her and hoped she would pick out something very sexy to try on. She obliged me by selecting some very froufrou fashions and asking me to come into the dressing room to help her with them.

The second we were inside, she stripped off everything she was wearing without any sign of embarrassment. I began to get the funny feeling that she was attracted to me in that same sexual way I was to her. She almost seemed to be flirting with me, taking every opportunity to have me look at her. She didn't rush into the things she had picked out, but just stood there naked, making small talk.

Finally, looking right into my eyes, she nodded toward a strapless bra she had brought in and asked me to help her into it. I could see that her nipples were as hard as rocks. I knew instinctively that this was going to be different than with the other women who shopped at my boutique. When I snapped the clasp at the back of the bra and reached inside the cup to adjust it, I felt my own nipples responding with erection.

Her breast was warm and silky to the touch. As I lifted and manipulated it inside the cup of the bra, the hardness of her nipple raked against the palm of my hand. When I looked at her in the mirror, my hand still on her breast, she had a sultry smile on her face. It was a smile that showed me she knew where I was at, and that she knew I knew where she was at. When I started to move my hand, she grabbed it firmly. Meeting my gaze in the mirror, she spoke softly. "Don't take your hand away. It feels too good," she said in a sexy voice.

I was startled and much too excited to move it away. So I cupped and squeezed it gently, allowing my fingers to knead into the softness of her breast. She stood there watching in the mirror and moaning softly. I took it upon myself to lower the bra to give me access to both her breasts. I filled my palms with her flesh and let my fingers stroke her nipples.

They were becoming larger and even harder than before. She was obviously enjoying every moment, and so, losing all my inhibitions, I took control. I began rolling her pink nipples between my fingers.

While I played with them, I became so aroused that I could feel my panties getting wet. Touching her breasts was driving me wild. I couldn't believe that my fantasy was actually becoming a reality. I couldn't believe that touching this woman was making me feel things I had never felt with a man.

Speaking into the mirror in a voice that was almost inaudible, she mouthed the words, "Suck my nipples." Then she closed her eyes. It was as though she had read my mind, because at that very moment I was wondering if I could take that liberty. My hands quickly pulled the bra from her body and tossed it to the floor.

My lips pressed against her nipple and for the first time in my life I tasted the sweet, salty savor of another woman's body. My tongue darted across the pink bud, making it wet and even more erect. I sucked hard until the swollen erection was buried in my mouth. She was moaning now, letting me know how much she was enjoying it. My own body was so stirred up that I felt like I was on fire. With my hand, I played with her other breast while my mouth kept up its exploration.

In the mirrors that lined the walls, I watched her whole body convulsing, twisting and turning, humping and gyrating in a sexual motion that was churning and driving my passions. Never before had I been so turned on, so filled with desire. I was touching her naked body, sucking her nipples, intimately exploring her, peering at her nakedness. Suddenly I realized I had wanted to do this to other women all my life.

With my free hand, I gently touched her pubic mound. It was beautiful and very hairy. She sighed when she felt my hand on her pussy. I kept having to ask myself if I was dreaming or was this really happening to me. It was too good to be true. My fingers rolled through her hairy bush and I summoned the thought of what it would feel like once my fingers got inside her vagina. I waited before I went any further, because the thoughts alone were almost overpowering me. She seemed willing to let me take all the time I wanted. It was making her hotter, too.

I could feel the lips of her pussy parting, liquid oozing out to wet the little curling hairs that surrounded her sex. I concentrated on pleasuring her, feeling my own body filling with pleasure at the same time. I could hear my heart thumping with excitement. Horny sensations were creeping all over me. She was pushing her hips toward me, almost as if they could talk and beg me to go further. All the time, I kept thinking about her pussy and what it was going to feel like once my fingers got inside. I savored every moment until I couldn't contain myself any longer.

Ever so slowly I gently spread her pussy lips apart with my finger and started to slip it inside her warm flowing vagina. I felt a thrill deep inside my own pussy as my finger slid deeper and deeper into her womanhood. She spread her legs wide to allow my access. I looked at the mirror and saw an expression of contented lewdness on her face mingled with the knowledge that I was feeling the same. Her pussy was so lubricated that my finger seemed to be swimming around deep inside her. As I fondled her, I could feel my own juices starting to escape from my own pussy lips.

Inside her vagina I felt folds and folds of softness lapping over my fingers. I moved my hand in a fucking motion, while her body pushed hard against its exploration. She was like a wild woman trying desperately to satisfy her sexual urges. Grunts of passion bubbled from her lips as her pelvis moved in time with my plunging finger. When I looked at her face in the mirror, she appeared transplanted into another world. I couldn't believe such ecstasy was possible between women.

As my finger rolled around inside her pussy, I moved my palm against her until it found her distended clitoris. It felt wonderful to touch her there. The more gentle pressure I applied, the bigger it grew. I bathed her clit in fluid carried from the inner folds of her vagina on the tip of my finger. Her gurgling sounds were getting louder, and her body moved with greater urgency. I couldn't tell which of us was more on fire or deriving more pleasure. It was absolutely amazing to me that this was happening.

I could feel my own clit getting larger and larger, until there was no doubt that I was moving toward orgasm without even being touched. Feeling her exaggerated the sensations within me. I had been playing with my own clit since I was in my early teens, but I never even imagined how exciting it would be to touch another woman's and to bring her the pleasure I had learned to give myself. I never wanted to stop and hoped that this feeling I was receiving would last forever and ever.

I could see in the mirror that she too was in a state of total erotic intoxication. Her eyes were closed and the expression on her face said it all. It was as though her pores themselves oozed ecstasy, the sheer pleasure of sexuality, the deep absorption in her passionate state.

Then with a soft erotic sigh, she murmured, "I'm coming, I'm coming." Her whole body tensed and recoiled with each gush of her orgasm. I could feel the steady flow of her climactic juices drenching my hand. It seemed like she was orgasming forever. Then, without even the slightest touch from my partner, my own orgasm was on me. I kept my finger moving on her clit as my eruption began. I knew that touching her was what had done this to me.

"I'm coming, too," I whispered. I was in a total trance, experiencing sensations I had never felt before. It was beautiful. The feeling of pleasure gushed and gushed until at long last the whirlwind of sensations subsided and I began to return to earth.

After the two of us had finished discharging the built-up sexual tension and had a chance to catch our breaths, we hugged each other for quite a while. That was the very first time I had ever experienced an orgasm of such magnitude and intensity. I had discovered a new me. I had finally found a source of sexual satisfaction.

Since then I have learned about the subtle exchange of signals that hungry women can use to invite each other's caresses. I have discovered that there are many women, like me, who lead unsatisfactory sex lives within their marriages and can find erotic fulfillment only with each other. My shop and the fresh erotic lifestyle it brings me has opened up new vistas. I am a much happier person for it. At last, in my boutique, I have an opportunity to be who I really am. I feel that Saunder has benefited from my new discovery too, because my contentment makes his life more comfortable.

OUT-OF-TOWN ADVENTURES

Benton is thirty-eight years of age and owns his own plumbing business. He is on the stocky side, with the beginnings of a potbelly. His height, just under five feet eight inches, makes him look heavier than he is. Benton has been shaving his head since he started to go bald. He says that if he did not, he would look unkempt. His hazel eyes are bright and alert. His gracious smile comes naturally. His skin is pale, probably because his work keeps him indoors and away from the sun. He has an easygoing nature and a conversational style that makes a person comfortable in his presence.

I grew up with plumbing in my veins, you might say. My family has a long history in the business. My grandfather was a plumber, and so was my father. For quite a while, we were the only game in town. When the community started to grow, with new houses popping up all over, our plumbing business really took off. My father was smart. He plowed some of the profits back into the business and invested the rest in real estate. Now the business is mine, and my wife and family are financially stable. I still plumb, of course, but I have six other guys working for me.

I was thirty years old when I married. Now I'm the proud daddy of two beautiful little girls. Before my marriage I dated a bit, but not much. I'm not what you would call a ladies' man. If anything, just the opposite. Even when I was in high school, girls were not one of my priorities. While all my friends were dating, or going out with their steady girls, I always found reasons for being too busy to date. For one thing, I worked in my dad's business. For another, I'm not exactly a rocket scientist. It always took lots of time and hard work just to keep from flunking my classes.

By the time I graduated from high school, I was already a journey-man plumber. My dad was proud of my abilities, but he was always pushing me to find a girl and settle down. When I went out with some-one, it was mainly to please him or my mother. Somehow, dating just seemed to be too much work. I didn't feel natural playing the game and making idle conversation while trying to grab a titty in the dark. I was much more comfortable with a wrench in my hand than a girl.

Eventually, my mom and a buddy of mine set up a date between me and Emma. She was my friend's cousin. We hit it off pretty nicely. Emma was as socially clumsy as I was. Maybe that's why we got along. Anyway, two years after that first date, we were married. It's been a good marriage, I guess. The sex is always satisfying. I never could understand why my friends seemed to be totally consumed with it, though. It's nice, but the earth don't move for me like they tell me it does for them.

Most of the guys I know cheat on their wives with other women. To hear them tell it, they've got insatiable sexual appetites and one woman just ain't enough. They seem to love talking about their con-quests and experiences. I just listen with half an ear, not all that interested, to tell you the truth. They're always making fun of me and telling me I don't know what I am missing.

They come up with all kinds of reasons why it's all right for them to cheat, how it improves their sexual abilities. Being with lots of dif-ferent women makes them better lovers, they say. In the end, their wives are better off for their extracurricular activities, they say. They got one excuse after another to defend what they do. They make me out to be a sucker, a goody-goody guy who believes what the preacher says on Sunday mornings.

I never told them, but the truth is I just have no desire or curiosity for any other women besides Emma. She's all I can handle. From what I hear them telling me, she and I don't have sex anywheres near as often as these guys do with their wives. Then they go out and have other women besides. I always just figured maybe I have a lower sex drive than them. It wasn't until a year ago that I found out there's more to the story than that.

I had went to the annual plumbing supply exhibition, as I usually do. For some reason, all the hotels I knew in the city where the convention was seemed to be booked. I had to stay in one of the expensive ones that I usually avoid. It isn't that I can't afford it. Hell, it's a tax deduction anyway. I just don't usually feel comfortable in those fancy places. Anyways, this time I had no choice.

The first night I was there, I was in the hotel's restaurant to have dinner, when I noticed a guy at another table looking at me. I looked back, trying to figure out if I knew him from somewhere. After a while, the gentleman walked over and introduced himself. I don't quite know how it happened, but we ended up sharing my table and eating together.

He was a salesman, attending some kind of sales convention at the hotel. We seemed to come from two different worlds, but we actually hit it off immediately. Conversation flowed pretty natural, and before I knew what was happening, we were having drinks together in his room. At first, I was very comfortable in his presence. But after a few drinks, I started to feel strange. This whole thing was affecting me in a way I never felt before. I couldn't understand it.

We were just having a normal conversation. But I felt like there was a fire deep in my body. It was almost like sexual passion, the kind I never really felt with my wife. While my new friend talked, my head was filling with all sorts of sex thoughts. No matter how hard I tried, I couldn't stop the weird images from coming.

I was actually picturing he and I doing all sorts of sexual things to each other. I was wondering what it would be like to have him touch my dick, or for me to touch his. These erotic thoughts, I guess you could call them, were making me very uncomfortable. What's worse, I had a hard-on. I mean a real whopper of a hard-on. My cock felt more rigid than an old galvanized pipe. It was so strange.

He wasn't coming on to me or flirting with me. He was acting perfectly normal. I could feel my face turning red from the twisted pornographic images that were running through my head. I had never felt this way with any woman—not even my wife! Now, out of nowhere, I was getting hard with this guy.

I was just thinking it was the alcohol, when he asked if I would refill his glass. I guess it was natural, because I was sitting a lot closer to the table with the setup on it than he was. I got all embarrassed, though, and couldn't for the life of me bring myself to get up. Sitting, I could hide my erection by keeping my hands in my lap. But once I was standing, he would notice my hard-on and I would be busted. What if he thought I was queer or something?

My new friend waited patiently, though, never moving out of his chair. I didn't know what else to do. There was no getting around it. I would have to oblige and fill his glass. I got up carefully, keeping my back to him as good as I could. While I was pouring, I heard him laugh out loud.

"What's so funny?" I asked, my back still to him.

"You don't have to hide your stiff cock," he said. My face felt like it caught on fire and I was burning up. I couldn't bring myself to look at him. "If you would turn around," he said, with that laugh still in his voice, "you'd see that I'm every bit as excited as you are."

My first thought was to get offended, though I really don't know why. I forced myself to bite the bullet and turn slowly to face him. He was getting out of his chair, and I could see that his cock was also hard and sticking straight out in front of him making a huge bulge in his pants. For a long moment, there was silence as we both stood looking at each other's erections. Then he walked towards me.

I guess I was acting on instinct, because without thinking or hesitating for an instant, we fell into each other's arms and actually started kissing. I could taste alcohol on his lips. Our tongues sampled each other as I felt his fingers unbuttoning my shirt. Part of me wanted to stop and shove him away. But a stronger part of me wanted this to continue.

Slowly he pulled away my shirt. Next, he went for my belt buckle, opened it up, and started working on the button of my pants. I did nothing. I was too excited and confused. I just let my arms hang down on my sides and let him do what he wanted. His fingers tugged at the zipper of my fly. When my pants fell open, they slid down to the floor around my ankles. I felt his fingers go to the waistband of my underwear, and he pulled them down until they joined my pants.

Letting him lead me forward, I stepped out of my clothing and stood as naked as the day I was born. I couldn't believe how sexy it felt. My cock was so hard that it sprang straight out and I could feel it throbbing. I watched my friend's eyes lower and glue themselves to my hard-on. I felt the palm of his hand circling the shaft of my cock. With his other hand he reached down and cupped my balls.

So slow it was almost painful, he started to pull the skin of my swollen cock up and down. I couldn't do anything but stare at the masturbating movements of his hand. My cock got harder and larger until the veins were a deep dark blue and a quivering movement stirred in them. His touch was strong yet gentle. My entire body felt thrills and chills like I never experienced before. I was so excited I could hardly contain myself. My eyes were fastened to his manipulating hands, watching in fascination as he stroked up and down.

I was so hot that I had to reach over and grab his hand to make him stop. "I'm too close to spilling my load," I said, not believing that it was my voice talking. His hand stopped moving, but he still held lightly on to my cock.

"Why don't you undress me?" he whispered. Not knowing what else to do but obey, I undid his pants. It excited me to pull down his zipper and then tug on his pants until they fell to the floor. Through his underwear, I saw his huge cock straining against the material. There was even a little wet spot where the tip of it was. I found that I couldn't wait to see what it looked like and to touch it.

Slowly, afraid of these new feelings, I began to lower his shorts until they joined his pants on the floor. I took a deep breath at the sight of his exposed hard-on. It was enormous. I had seen other guy's cocks before, but they never had an effect on me like this. His was huge. "Wow," I said, "I can't believe what I'm doing." Then, flustered and confused I sputtered, "You have a beautiful cock. It's immense." My words made it twitch.

He smiled at my dazzled eyes. "Touch it," he whispered.

I reached out and took it into my hand. It felt even larger than it looked. The skin of his erection felt soft and smooth, as though I was feeling the essence of satin. It was hot to the touch. Like an animal with a life of its own, it started to bob up and down against the palm of my hand. It was so large that I was able to get both my hands around his swollen shaft.

Touching this other man's dick gave me all kinds of erotic feelings like I never felt before. My hands worked feverishly up and down and all around his aroused hard-on until I felt the veins of it stand away from the sheath. I was on fire. Just the mere thought of my hands rubbing a cock was making me shiver. It was unbelievable.

He began stroking my cock again, the same way I was rubbing his. We stood facing each other, exchanging pleasures that almost swept me off my feet. Our hips moved in circles that added even more to the thrilling sense I was feeling. It was a brand-new sexual phenomenon, like a starship visit to a planet I never seen before.

Together, we rollicked, our bodies moving back and forth in a flaming exchange of passion. I could hear groans of ecstasy and wasn't sure whether they were coming from him or me. I'm telling you, we must of sounded like a choir of sex. I could feel my body tensing and realized I was about to come. I was afraid, but there was nothing I could do to stop it. Just as I was ready to bust, I felt his erection begin to jerk and tighten.

It was absolutely amazing. The two of us were having climaxes at the very same time. Never before had I experienced that. Me and Emma never come together. I watched spurt after spurt of hot white fluid shoot out from the tip of his cock. I even found the sight of it exciting. I let my hands get covered with his goo and I watched as my own cock gushed. Our bodies moved in time with each blast that erupted from our swollen cock heads.

When every last drop had been emptied, I thought it was over. But he put his arms around me and I found us embracing like a pair of lovers. We even kissed each other passionately.

The whole thing was an experience I will never forget. I guess you could say it was the thrill of a lifetime for me. We laid down on the bed together and rested in silence for a while before a word was spoken. I wanted to let him know that I never had sex with a man before and never imagined that I could be queer. After all, I was married with children. Until now, the thought of having sex with another man was as foreign to me as anything. I tried to tell him how confused I was, how scared.

He listened to every word I said and waited until I emptied my brain of its fear. Then he opened up and told me he didn't think either of us were queer. "I'm also a married man," he said. "I also never tried another man until after I was married. Then, it happened pretty much the way it happened for you. It came as a total surprise. For a while, I couldn't come to terms with the possibility that I might prefer men to women. But now that I know it, it's fine with me."

He told me he was still happily married, but every now and then needed to satisfy a sexual urge that can only be fulfilled by another man. He only allows himself to do that when he's away on business. He said it helps keep his home life normal. He even told me that his wife knows all about it and has no objections as long as he stays away from other women.

He said he didn't think it meant that he was queer or gay, and he didn't think it meant that I was either. From what he told me, I think most gays know about their preference for other males at an early age, even though they don't always let themselves experience it. In the case of guys like he and I, it's just something we need once in a while. It even can make our marriages stronger. Well, I don't know about that, but the things he said helped me not feel guilty for having a sexual encounter with him.

Since that experience, I've done pretty much what he does. I stick to the straight and narrow while I'm at home, but if I happen to be out of town on business, I go looking for another guy. Funny, now that I know what I'm looking for, it's never hard to find it. It only happens every few months. I find myself in bed with a man, having the kind of wild and exciting sex that has never been possible with Emma. Then I go home to her and our life stays happy. Maybe someday, I'll follow my first male partner's lead and tell her all about it. Maybe it will be all right with her, like it is for that other guy's wife. But to tell you the truth, I can't really imagine telling her.

I've learned to live my erotic lifestyle in a quiet sort of way. I don't feel guilty, because I'm not running around with any other women or cheating in the usual sense of the word. I'm not even sure that playing with another guy's dick and letting him play with mine counts as adultery. Except for that sort of thing, my sex is exclusive with my wife. I'm just glad I finally discovered myself and have been able to find out why sex is such a big deal.

11

HAVE A GOOD TIME, DEAR

WHEN ELEPHANT SEAL FEMALES ARE IN HEAT, A SINGLE male, known to animal behaviorists as the beachmaster, fights jealously to isolate his harem of up to fifty females from all the other sex-hungry males on the beach. As a result, only the biggest, strongest, fiercest males succeed in breeding and passing their genes along to the next generation. In this way, sexual jealousy serves the useful function of improving the herd by assuring that only the fittest will reproduce. The same behavior can be seen in many other animal species and probably existed among human beings at some point in our evolution.

There is some disagreement among philosophers, psychologists, anthropologists, and other students of the human condition about whether sexual jealousy serves any useful function for us now, however. Some argue that it continues to provide a motivator that strengthens the stability of the family unit. Others assert that the need for jealousy has passed and that our race would be better off without it.

We will leave the answer to those who devote their careers to such questions. As observers, we can say only that jealousy is an emotion common to most of the people we have interviewed. In a marriage or other domestic partnership, it can lead to problems that may escalate from minor arguments to bitter fights, to divorce, even to violence and murder.

A few people have managed to eliminate sexual jealousy from their relationships. Not only do they accept their partners' erotic contacts with outsiders, but they draw pleasure and excitement from witnessing those contacts. Their stories are told in this chapter.

WATCHING GRETTA

Kyle is forty-seven years old but looks more like a man in his thirties. He's an eighth of an inch short of six-foot-two, with a muscular yet slender physique. He has a beautiful head of thick black hair, the kind that makes women want to run their fingers through it. His saucer eyes are almost as dark as the hair on his head. They look young and vibrant and flash a kind of glittering light as he speaks. His hands move about as though they were doing the talking. His facial expressions are animated and dynamic. His thick lips move dramatically while he speaks, revealing perfectly straight white teeth. His complexion is flawless. His skin color is olive with a soft sheen reminiscent of satin.

I'm a comedian by profession and have been in show business for nearly twenty years now. I love making people laugh. And I love being on the road. I do a lot of traveling in my business. It keeps life interesting and the scenery constantly changing. Going from city to city is a learning experience. It teaches me all kinds of things. But I never thought I'd be learning lessons from a woman half my age.

When I was younger, I fell into the trap of getting married. It didn't last very long. Jealousy was what broke us up. Her jealousy and mine. If she caught me so much as looking at another woman, she'd fly into a rage. I was the same way. If I thought her skirt was showing a little too much leg, I'd get so pissed I'd rant and rave for hours. As a result, we were always fighting. Finally, after a year, we got a divorce and went our separate ways.

After that, I stayed away from serious relationships. I guess I figured if I kept it light, that green-eyed monster would never rear its ugly head. I missed a lot that way, although I didn't find it out until I was forty. Then I met Gretta. She was only nineteen. That didn't make any difference to me, since I had no intention of getting involved. All I had in mind was a little fun. I thought a man of my experience would be able to show her a thing or two. Boy, did I have that backwards.

For some reason, women are usually pretty impressed when I tell them I'm in show business, so I've always worked that to help me pick them up. It's how I started in with Gretta. She was waiting tables in a coffee shop near a theater where I was performing. It wasn't much of a gig. Flesh was the main attraction. They were just using the comedy to make it legitimate. I did fifteen- or twenty-minute sets between strippers.

Anyway, when I took a table at the coffee shop and Gretta came over to take my order, I thought she might be good for a night's entertainment. She had red hair and a tight little body with curves that strained the buttons of her waitress uniform. I could see the outline of her nipples against the material, and the skirt was short enough to show plenty of her firm young legs.

I gave her my order and said, "I'm appearing at the theater down the street, and I go on in an hour, so I'm in a bit of a hurry." I expected that to get her attention, and it did.

"Oh," she said. "You're an entertainer? Wow." She walked away, but when she came back with my food, she had more to say. "I thought that was a striptease place," she said. "I didn't know they had male strippers, too."

I laughed. "No," I explained. "I'm a comedian. The folks are really coming to see me. The strippers are just there to fill the time between my acts."

Now it was her turn to laugh. It was nice and musical. "I've always wanted to see professional strippers work," she said, sort of wistfully. "But I never felt comfortable about going in there."

"Well," I answered. "Why don't you come and see my show? Just think of the strippers as something you have to sit through while you're waiting." I pulled out one of the complimentary tickets the theater gave me for promotional purposes and handed it to her. "Come as my guest. Stop off and see me in my dressing room."

I wasn't sure whether she'd take the ticket, but she did without hesitation. "Okay, I'll do that," she said with a smile. Then she walked off to the kitchen. I wondered what she meant when she made that remark about watching professional strippers, but I put it out of my head, ate my lunch, and went to the theater.

I had almost forgotten about the incident when I noticed her in the audience during my act. The theater was half empty, and most of the people there were men, so I couldn't miss her. I felt pretty good about her coming to see me and was sure it meant she was a plum ripe for plucking. Back in my dressing room, I waited for her knock at the door, but it was a good forty minutes before she came.

As soon as she entered the room, she thanked me for the ticket. "What a great show," she said exuberantly.

"Glad you liked it," I answered, trying to be humble. "Which part did you like best?" Of course, I meant which of my jokes was the funniest. I was in for a surprise.

"I liked the cowgirl," she said. "Great costume, and very nice moves." When I realized she was talking about one of the strippers, I was taken aback. I was even more startled when she added, "But I think I'm better."

Out front, the band was playing for another stripper, and the music could clearly be heard in my dressing room. To my amazement, she began swaying to it, saying, "Here, let me show you what I can do." Slowly, she unbuttoned the front of the waitress uniform that she was still wearing. As it opened, a lacy black bra and matching panties were revealed. She shed the dress and danced for a while in her underwear. Then, with graceful movements of her hands, she unsnapped the front of the bra and began to open it, holding it in a way that continued to cover her full breasts. Little by little, she exposed them to me, until even the hard pink nipples were showing. Then, tossing the bra to one side, she began removing the panties. When the red hair of her bush came into sight, I couldn't stand it any longer.

I tore my own clothes off and moved towards her, reaching out to take her in my arms. She melted into me, pressing her naked body against mine. I could feel her nipples drilling into my chest and her pelvis grinding against me. Somehow, my cock found her pussy without help, and within seconds I was inside her. I lifted her gently, and she wrapped her legs around mine, forcing my cock all the way in. We rolled against each other for a few minutes until I felt my balls churning with climax. She was young, but she had plenty of experience. She knew how close I was getting.

"Don't hold back," she whispered. "Come in me. I'll come with you." With that, we both began the contractions of orgasm. I felt like I was pumping all I had into her as she welded herself tightly to me.

After we cleaned ourselves up, she went back to the audience, and I went out to do another routine. When the show was over, she came back to my hotel with me, and we spent the night fucking. It was fantastic. The next night, we got together again. And the night after that. I was booked into that theater for two weeks, and I was starting to think of us as a couple. But the fourth night, she told me she wouldn't be coming to my hotel, because she had a date with another guy.

Even though I had been telling myself that there was nothing serious about my relationship with her, those old feelings of jealousy started to rise within me. "What?" I said angrily. "You're breaking a date with me to go out with someone else? Like hell!"

She giggled and then laughed raucously. "Why, it sounds like you're jealous," she said incredulously. "That's the dumbest thing I ever heard. I thought you were grown-up."

I felt a little foolish. "I am grown-up," I said. "But I like you, and

I hate the idea of you being with anyone else. You aren't going to fuck him, are you?"

She laughed some more. "Of course I am, silly," she answered. "But that has nothing to do with you. In fact, if you're in your room around ten or so tonight, I'll come and fuck you after I'm finished fucking him." She trailed a finger along the front of my pants, toying with my stiffening cock. "How would that be?"

I didn't know what to say. I was still feeling jealous, but her promise to come over and fuck me after fucking him was just weird enough to appeal to me. I looked down and said, "Well, I might be. If something else doesn't come along." I was hoping that remark would make her feel some of the jealousy I was feeling, but she only shrugged.

That night, I paced the floor of my hotel room nervously, torn between anger about the idea of her fucking someone else, and excitement at the thought of her coming to my room all hot from that and ready for more. By ten-fifteen, I was beginning to think it wasn't going to happen. By ten-thirty, I had given up. Then, around ten forty-five, there was a soft knock at the door. I went to it, prepared to give her hell for being late, but when I opened it, I just stood there with my mouth open.

There were two men and a woman with her. They walked into the room without a word and Gretta closed the door behind them. "This is Maggie," she said. "If you're good, you may get to fuck her and me both."

I just stared. Maggie was short and meaty. Plenty of flesh in all the right places, especially in the ass department. She wore a skimpy tube top that was much too tight for her plump body. It squashed her titties flat inside its confines. Her skirt was real short, revealing much of her ample thighs. For a moment, I forgot about the other men. I couldn't wait to see Maggie naked and in action.

Then Gretta introduced me to the guys. One had brown hair in a crewcut and the other had dirty blond hair in one long, neat braid that hung halfway down his back. Let's just call the first one Crew and the other one Pony, because in all honesty, I really can't remember their names.

I was feeling tense, but I tried to hide it. The five of us sat around on the couch, chairs, and the edge of the bed. They had brought beer and pot, so we drank a bit and smoked a few joints. I had no idea where this was going to go and didn't know what to say.

After a while, Gretta broke the ice. She turned on the radio and twirled the dial until she found some heavy-metal rock. Then, stepping into the center of the room, she began a slow and sexy striptease. I was numb. Even though I had only known her a short time, seeing her undress in front of the others was making me feel jealous. But she kept right on. The two guys whistled and clapped while Gretta stripped, and I tried to join the fun by doing some clapping myself. Finally, there was nothing left for her to take off.

As Gretta continued dancing, totally nude, Maggie jumped up from the couch and proceeded to do a strip of her own. When she peeled off her tube top, the softest, fleshiest tits I had ever seen popped out and bobbed up and down. I wanted to reach out and grab them in my hands, but I settled for devouring her with my eyes. I was so turned on watching Maggie, that I completely forgot my jealous feelings about Gretta. The two guys undressed quickly and without even thinking about it, I did too.

Gretta boldly walked over to Crew and took hold of his head, pressing his face into her warm boobies. He knew exactly what to do and started kissing and licking her tits, making wet slurping sounds of pleasure. Everyone watched as Gretta's nipples grew bigger and harder. Pony got up from his seat and walked around until he stood at Gretta's back. She enticed him by spreading her legs and shoving her ass out at him. He had his hand on his cock and was rubbing it up and down. The more he rubbed the darker the color got on its head, until it turned deep blue. I could see the veins running up and down the length of his shaft pulsating under the skin. I couldn't believe how huge it had grown. Keeping a firm grip on his dick, Pony worked it inside of Gretta's wet pussy from behind.

Maggie was sitting beside me on the couch now, both of us naked. Together, we watched with great excitement as Crew sucked hard on Gretta's nipples and Pony's cock was being swallowed by her pussy. When it had completely disappeared inside, I heard Gretta gasp with excitement.

Maggie looked over at me and reached for my cock. It was already hard, but Maggie's hand caressing it was making it even harder. She petted my cock until it reached mammoth size, bigger than I ever remember it being. Anyway, that's how it seemed. Her hand moved gently, lightly, making me love every second of her touch. When I was throbbing with desire, she got on her knees between my open legs, bent her naked body over my lap, and swallowed up my throbbing hard-on.

Her mouth felt hot as her tongue slid up and down my pulsating cock. She spread the saliva from her mouth until my cock was swimming in it. Her tongue danced around the head and I could feel the rim palpitating with each long, lapping stroke. In a flash, I realized that watching two men fucking Gretta wasn't making me jealous anymore. It was turning me on, increasing the excitement of everything Maggie was doing.

When my chubby partner let my drenched cock pop out of her mouth, I was disappointed. But immediately, she picked herself up from the floor and sat on my lap with her back to me. Just before her ass came to rest on my thighs, she took hold of my swollen dick and placed it between her pussy lips. As she lowered her soft fleshy ass onto my lap, my hard-on slipped easily inside her.

Maggie turned her head slightly and whispered, "This way we can both watch Gretta and the boys get it on while you fuck me."

"Good idea," I answered, before I even realized I was saying it. The conquest of my jealousy was complete. My eyes glued to the writhing spectacle of Gretta and her two lovers, I reached around and took hold of Maggie's luscious tits. Maggie bounced up and down on my ever-ready cock, her pussy gliding easily with the abundance of feminine fluid that flowed inside her box.

My fingers and hands got lost in the flesh of her breasts. It was like squeezing mounds of soft fluffy cotton. Her nipples grew hard and long as I massaged and kneaded them. Fucking Maggie and playing with her tits was great, but what made it even hotter was watching Gretta getting fucked from behind by one man while another sucked her tits. It didn't take me long to reach the apex of my orgasm. I just couldn't hold it back. Before my cock had a chance to spout, Maggie was screaming with excitement. She was coming. I could feel her tight channel convulsing around my shaft. There was no need to wait. I came with her.

Gretta was next. Just when my orgasm was coming to its end, she began making the sounds of passion I had learned to recognize as her climax. Moments later Pony began grunting, as he pumped his cum into my young girlfriend's body. Crew was still sucking Gretta's nipples, his hand moving furiously on his own swollen cock.

Suddenly Maggie's body left my lap. She jumped on Crew and wrestled him to the ground, mounting and straddling him. I watched as she took his cock in her hand and put it where mine had just left a load. I thought of my wet cum greasing her pussy for another man as his cock slipped easily into her.

As soon as he was all the way in, her provocative ass began to bounce up and down on Crew's hard-on. She rode him like a bucking bronco, never breaking the rhythm of her frantic movements. I was so turned on watching Maggie's bobbing ass and those large fleshy tits hanging down that my cock was starting to tingle and rise all over again. When Crew's body started to tighten and then slacken I knew he was only moments away from catching up to the rest of us. Then, as if to make sure that we were all in on it with him, he yelled in a voice that demanded attention, "Oh, I'm coming!" He was squeezing Maggie's big ass so hard, he left fingerprints.

A little later, when all of us were basking calmly in the afterglow of sexual satisfaction, Gretta lay down on the floor, spread her legs real wide, and started to masturbate. Pony handed me a beer, and we all sat and drank, watching the sensual show that Gretta was so erotically giving us. She spread her pussylips apart with her fingers, making sure that we all had a good clear view of her hot, wet interior. The lips were dark pink and coated with a glistening goo. The more she played with the inside of her labia, the wetter they became, until the large button of her clit was showing.

My eyes moved from her open pussy to the expression on her face. She was playing with the pleasure-button now and enjoying every sensation she was able to give herself. To my surprise, Maggie joined her on the floor and started to lick Gretta's opening. I was instantly hard. I couldn't help stealing a look at Crew and Pony and saw that they were erect also. Crew was rubbing his cock again, as he had done before.

The three of us watched Maggie's tongue go from deep inside Gretta's pussy to the puckering tent around her clit. I've never seen a bigger clit than Gretta's that night. Within minutes, she went on to her next orgasm. She purred and aahed while every last drop of fluid flowed from her gyrating body. Maggie kept licking her, until Pony got up, bent over her, took her hips in his hands, and rolled her over onto her back.

He climbed on top of her while she spread her thighs to accommodate his enlarged cock. We all watched it disappear deep inside Maggie's pussy. We groaned and moaned with them as it slid in and out of her. Each time we got a view of his shaft sliding outwards, it was wetter than before.

Gretta motioned for Crew to come and join her on the floor. She stayed on her back and spread her legs wide to invite Crew's cock inside. The two couples moved simultaneously in perfect synchronization.

Everybody was fucking but me, but that didn't bother me at all. It was making me excited to watch Gretta have sex with another man, and the sight of Maggie and her partner was adding to the excitement. I played with my hard-on while my eyes went from one couple to the next. It was extremely arousing to see the cocks sliding in and out so effortlessly. I could hear the sound of each guy's body slapping down against his woman's mound. It's a sound that only comes from fucking. Each time one of the guys would raise his pelvis, his cock came into sight, dripping wet.

As the two men pumped deep and hard into their partners' openings, I watched the muscles in their asses tighten and contract. Even that turned me on. They fucked for a long time before any one of them was able to come again. The longer it took, the more the women enjoyed it. They were loving the way they were being banged hard and fast. Finally, I brought myself off, my cum shooting through the air as I enjoyed the visual spectacle unfolding before me.

We kept it up all night long, changing partners, doubling up, watching each other, and masturbating. I saw Gretta getting fucked in every possible position and by every possible combination of partners. The sight of her having sex with the others became the spicy aphrodisiac that kept my cock hard and my balls pumping. By the time morning came, my whole attitude toward my sex partners had changed.

I spent the rest of my stay in that city with Gretta, and we got together with Crew, Pony, and Maggie twice more after that first time. I learned to love watching a woman I had a relationship with screwing other men. When I moved on, Gretta and I said we would stay in touch, but when I tried calling her, I found she had moved. I never heard from her again.

Even though short, the time I spent with her and the lesson she taught me has stayed with me. Now I don't even bother with a woman unless she's willing to let me watch her having sex with someone else. Sometimes, it's a group thing, where I get to fuck someone also. Other times, I just jerk off while I watch my partner with another man, or occasionally with a woman. I find watching her do it with another even more exciting that having her do it with me.

The funny thing is, I've never had trouble finding women who are willing. In fact, I think that telling a woman early in the game that I go for that sort of thing makes it easier to connect. Now, it's so much a part of my life, that I can't imagine going back to the old vanilla sex.

LAS VEGAS ESCORT

Justine just turned twenty-nine and says she still feels young, vibrant, and as sexy as she felt when she was eighteen. She stands five feet nine inches tall, holds herself in an erect position, and takes great pride in her figure. Justine says that if it weren't for her large breasts she could have had a future in modeling, and maybe she is right. She is light-skinned, with bright green eyes and golden blond hair cut in a stylishly short bob. Her friendly and bubbly personality makes one like her immediately. She is in sales and claims to be one of her company's highest achievers. Justine says she is a newlywed, married just a little over a year.

Although we are only recently married, my husband and I have been a couple, maybe an odd couple, since our college days. Martin was just starting his second year, and I my first. From the instant I saw him, I wanted to take him to bed. I know he felt the same way, because it didn't take more than two days for me to succeed. But even though he is and always was the best sex partner I ever had, I say we were an odd couple, because ordinary screwing has never been enough for either of us.

For the first several years of our relationships, we refused to think of ourselves as committed in any way. I had sex with lots of other people, and so did he. Sometimes, we even talked to each other about those experiences. Hearing him tell me about women he had fucked and describing the details of what he'd done to them and what they'd done to him didn't bother me at all. In fact, it turned me on. It seemed to turn him on when I described my adventures to him, too. But, still, we thought of ourselves as nothing more than casual sex partners. We were both afraid that if we gave our relationship a name, or even recognized that it was a relationship, we'd be restricted, and neither of us wanted that to happen.

We both feared an exclusive arrangement. Each of us wanted our own independence, to feel free to have sex with whomever we chose. It wasn't until a trip to Las Vegas that we realized we could be a couple and still keep ourselves open to other partners. If it hadn't been for that trip, I don't think we ever would have gotten married. It led to one of the most dramatic and stimulating experiences I ever had and was the beginning of a gloriously erotic lifestyle.

It started one afternoon about two years ago. We were in bed together and had been fucking for what seemed like hours. Just when I thought I was all sexed out, I had Martin tell me all about a scene he had done with one of his other women, and in no time I was hot again. The more he talked about her pussy and how he had used his tongue on it, the more I wanted him inside me. He could see the effect it was having on me. "You like thinking about me with another woman, don't you?" he teased.

"Yes," I admitted. "It makes me very hot." Just then I came, and he did too.

Afterwards, he asked me to join him on a trip to Las Vegas. He had a business conference there the following week. He knew that in my work as a sales rep, I can always steal away for a few days. He had a taunting look in his eyes when he said, "Maybe we can do something interesting there." I had no idea what he meant, but the way he said it was enough to make me curious. So I agreed to go.

Our city is only about four hours' drive from Vegas, so we went in his car. As we drove, we took turns telling each other about some of the sexual things we had done with other people. At one point, we both got so excited that we drove off onto a little dirt road that crossed the desert and got out to fuck standing up right out in the open.

He had made a reservation at one of the newer hotels on the Las Vegas strip. The room was fabulous—the deluxe kind that is usually reserved for high rollers. It was lavish, with every amenity you can imagine, including twin bathrooms with a phone and TV in each of them. As soon as we got in, we hit the king-size bed for a long, slow fuck. Then we went out onto the strip to absorb some of the Las Vegas excitement.

As we walked around, Martin kept taking newspapers out of racks on the street. I didn't pay much attention. But when we got back to the room, he spread them out on the bed and I realized they were advertisements for escort services. I was wondering what he had in mind, when he said, "Okay, why don't we pick one of these and get me a date. You can watch me with her. Should be even more exciting than descriptions."

The idea sounded so hot that I didn't hesitate for a moment. "I won't join in," I said. "But I'd love to see you in action."

We read the various ads and tried to pick one that didn't look too sleazy. When Martin phoned, he said nothing about me watching. He just arranged to have an escort come to our hotel. I found myself getting quite nervous at the thought. And very aroused.

About an hour later there was a knock at the door and a beautiful young woman showed up. When she stepped into the room, she looked from Martin to me and back again. "Couple?" she said. "Nobody told me that."

We explained that I was only going to watch. She said she was perfectly comfortable with the arrangement. She added that so many people come to Vegas with so many different sexual preferences that nothing surprised her. But although she had been working for this escort service for a couple of years, and wasn't at all shocked by our request, it was the first time anyone wanted that particular act.

The first thing she did was take care of business. She said that knowing I would be watching them would probably be a turn-on for her, but it was still going to cost a bit extra. Martin just smiled and paid what she asked. She tucked the cash in her purse and shook his hand and then mine. She said her name was Venus.

I don't know whether it was her appearance or her matter-of-fact response to our request, but I found it sexually exciting to look at her. I'd say she was in her early twenties. She had dark, curly brown hair that hung loose to her shoulders with dark eyes to match. She was of medium height with a body to die for. I guess in her profession she had to keep herself looking attractive and fit.

Venus was dressed in a black tight-fitting dress that came well above her knees. She wore high black heels that accentuated her slender legs and black panty hose to match. As soon as the financial business was concluded, she began to undress. First she removed her shoes. Standing barefoot in her stockings, she walked over toward where Martin was sitting on the bed and asked him to unzip her dress. Once he obliged, she stepped out of it and stood before us in her panty hose and bra.

The hose were dark, but she had no panties under them, and I could see the triangle of her pubic shadow peeking through. The bra was lacy and exposed just a bit of her rosy nipples. Ever so slowly she reached behind her and undid the bra's catch, letting her beautiful full breasts stand straight and tall before her. They were perfect. The sight of them brought an involuntary gasp from my throat.

I looked over at Martin and found him looking back at me. I tried to read his expression. His eyes said, "Isn't she something else?" But there was also a touch of uncertainty. He wanted to be sure this was still all right with me. To show him that it was, I licked my lips and ran my hands over my own body, nodding slightly.

Slowly and decisively, Venus began lowering her pantyhose to expose a perfectly flat tummy and flared hips. She bent at the waist to roll the last few inches over her ankles and off her dainty feet, pointing her smooth round ass in my direction. When she was totally naked, she looked even more beautiful than she had when clothed.

I sat in a chair that was placed beside the king-size bed and watched Martin undressing himself. I had seen his body hundreds of times before, but the situation seemed to heighten his masculinity. His broad chest looked powerful, and his cock was bigger than I had ever seen it. Fully naked, he walked over to where Venus was standing and put his hands on her tits. He fondled them and toyed with her nipples, glancing at me to assure himself that I was watching.

All I could do was stare at her bright pink nipples, seeing them grow until they stood out like big luscious strawberries, ripe and juicy and yearning to be plucked. I could imagine what Martin was feeling, and at the same time what she was feeling. Experimentally, I stroked my own breasts through the material of my blouse. My nipples were growing too, pushing tightly against the bra that contained them.

Venus moaned softly, her eyes slightly closed, taking in all the pleasure that Martin's hands and fingers were giving her. Her hips swayed from side to side and then from front to back. Watching her gyrating hips and hearing the sounds of pleasure escaping from her lips were churning my own passions. I never imagined how exciting this would be. Martin, too, was moving his pelvis, pressing his swollen cock against her hairy mound while his hands roamed freely over her lovely breasts and large erect nipples. As his body swayed with hers, I could almost feel his passionate exhilaration.

His eyes moved back and forth between my face and her breasts. I tried to feel what he was feeling, the sensation of making love to one person while another watched. Just the thought of what he was experiencing made me hotter. Probably that showed on my face, because every time he looked at me, he seemed to get more aroused. I felt a tingle running over my own nipples as I saw Martin's lips brush her pink nubs.

His lips puckered softly around one and then the other until he appeared to be swallowing them up in his mouth. When his lips parted and Venus's nipples slipped from within the confines of his mouth, I choked with excitement. They were now hot red instead of the soft pink of just a few moments ago. They were longer and harder, with a glistening sheen that bounced the light right into my eyes. As the color morphed from strawberry to a deep cherry, her tits spoke of the sheer essence of hot torrid sex.

I was loving this. Their naked bodies were standing together, moving in synchronization in the dance of the fucking motion. Sounds of passion were issuing harmoniously from their lips. I was so turned on that my nipples were palpitating with excitement, and the crotch of my panties was beginning to feel damp between my legs. As I watched, Martin manipulated Venus onto the bed on her back with her breasts and nipples pointing straight up at the ceiling above.

Martin was standing next to the bed, looking down at his play-mate. His dick was as hard as a rock and stood straight out in front of him. If it could speak, it would have been saying, "Touch me. Please touch me."

Venus heard its plea. She knew exactly what her partner needed and raised her arm to accommodate Martin's desire. She took his hard-on lovingly in one hand and wrapped her fingers gently around it. Ever so slowly, carefully, and precisely, she started to jerk it up and down. With her other hand, she began to cuddle his dangling scro-tum. Cupping it softly, her fingers massaged methodically, stroking the skin and tenderly kneading his balls. The groans of passion, the cooing and oohing that came from his throat, lifted me to an even more excited state.

My clothes were beginning to constrict me. It was amazing what an effect the sight before me was having on my body. Every move-ment that Venus made caused a tremor of excitement to run through me, like a bolt of lightning striking hard and fast. It was as though I was being touched myself, but in some ways this felt even better. I had held Martin's cock, and I had played with his balls. But I had never really been able to concentrate on how he looked while I played with him. Now, sitting quietly in my chair, I was a spectator to his pleasure.

After giving Martin's cock and balls as much attention with her hands as he could stand, Venus sat up and took his giant cock into her mouth. I watched as she delicately ran her lips and tongue up and down his swollen shaft. I could almost feel my lover's excitement building, communicating itself to my own feverish body. Chills ran up and down my back and thighs as I saw his face contort in total ecstasy.

By now, my own sexual needs were crying for satisfaction. I quickly got out of my skirt, blouse, and bra and sat for another minute in my wet panties. Then, leaning back in the chair, I pulled the damp garment down and kicked it onto the carpeted floor. Spreading my legs wide and wasting no more time, I gently inserted my middle finger in my hungry wet pussy and started to finger-fuck myself. It excited me especially to know that Martin and his partner could see me whenever they cared to look in my direction.

At first I pushed my finger in and out of my wanton pussy until I was nearly drowning in my own fluids. Then, when I was thoroughly soaked inside, my finger spread the moisture over my ever-growing clitoris. My passionate body was on fire and the more I touched and rubbed my clit, the larger and harder it grew. With my other hand, my fingers rolled hard and fast at my own churning nipples. Simultaneously, one hand finger-fucked my pussy and the other toyed with my nipples. As I pleasured myself, my eyes never left the sexual show that was going on in our room.

Venus was sucking furiously at Martin's cock now, while both her hands busied themselves with his heavy dangling scrotum. Martin's eyes were shut tight, and the expression on his face spoke of the delight and sexual bliss that Venus was giving him. I knew that he could hold out a long time before climbing to an orgasm. Sometimes I thought of Martin not as a human, but more like a fucking machine that once plugged in could go forever. I was glad, because I wanted this show to go on and on and on.

Venus never stopped. She kept her lips and tongue working like the pro she was. Every few seconds, she would look up at Martin's face and then stare directly between my legs to watch me pleasuring myself. I kept them spread real wide, wanting her to have a good look at my pussy. I performed for her, diddling myself frantically, as my other hand plucked at my hard red nipples. Watching her watch me and then watching Martin kicked my passion up another notch, more than even I thought was possible.

My finger worked hard and fast at my clit until it brought me to the brink of my own exploding orgasm. As soon as it started to wash all over my body, I gasped out loud that I was about to explode. Martin opened his eyes and looked toward where I was sitting. I could see him watching my fingers rolling furiously inside my pussy and satisfying my nipple craving. I started to scream with ecstasy and saw

Venus staring between my legs. Having them see me come was as exciting as watching them.

After my climax floated to a slow halt, I could still hear cries of pleasure coming from Martin's mouth. He was staring straight into my eyes with the glazed look of lust all over his face. I knew that seeing me come had carried him to the top. "I'm going to come!" he yelled. "I'm going to come in your mouth, Venus. Ooh, baby, I'm going to come in her mouth. Watch me. Watch me. I'm coming in her mouth."

Venus answered by working her tongue and lips even more vigorously. I saw Martin tighten and then relax, tighten and relax, as his twitching body convulsed in the delirious rhythms of climax. Back and forth he rolled until he poured every ounce of his semen into his obliging partner's throat.

Venus kept up a quick and steady movement until Martin's penis was spent. Only when it had shrunk back to its normal size did she let it slip out from inside her mouth. "That was great," Martin sighed, looking from my eyes, to Venus's eyes, and then back again. "Now it's your turn, Venus."

Venus smiled at each of us. "Okay," she said. "Now I'm finished working. Usually this is when I leave. But the two of you have me so turned on I couldn't possibly go without having you get me off."

She lay back down, and Martin sat beside her on the bed. Spreading her legs wide so I could see, he completely exposed her pussy to my view. Her mound was covered with thick dark hair, and I could see the delicate pink tissues of her labia. She was every bit as wet as I was, actually dripping with fluid. I could see droplets spotting the sheet. The sight began to arouse me all over again. I had seen her suck him until he came. Now I was going to see him bring her to orgasm. My pussy was tingling.

Martin was staring into my eyes and, from his facial expression, I could tell that he knew how turned on I was. I spread my legs again, exposing my own pussy for them to see. Once more, I began fingerfucking myself. Looking into Venus's open pussy had me all fired up.

My pussy was lubricating rapidly. I spread the gooey substance over my clit and began rolling it in gentle circles until it grew harder and bigger than ever.

As I masturbated, I watched Martin push his finger deep inside Venus's slit. It was so wet that it seemed to suck him right in. I couldn't tear my eyes away from the spectacle of her open sex. Each time Martin's finger slid out, her pussy turned into quicksand and sucked it deep inside again. His finger shimmered with the prostitute's womanly fluids. I could hear the sounds of wetness as he drove it in and out. The erotic music was driving me wild.

The wetter and hotter she got, the more I could see inside her. I was lost in the sight of all those folds and curlicues of rosy red membrane covered with the fragrant fluid of her hunger. The more Martin fingered her opening, the bigger her clit became until it popped out from high up between her pussy lips. I watched it transform from a tiny red presence to a burgeoning bubble.

Venus moved her hips to press her ass hard against the mattress, keeping up with the movements of Martin's plunging finger. Her eyes opened and closed as she looked from him to me and back again on an erotic roller coaster. Just when she began to moan, Martin's other hand went to her begging clit. The second she felt his touch, she groaned with delight.

I groaned with her. The sight of my lover's hands on Venus's pussy sent chills and thrills down my spine. I was so excited I felt like exploding all over again. I couldn't tear my eyes away from her huge clit, so big and beautiful. I almost felt I was touching it myself. I matched the motions of my hand on my own clitoris to Martin's busy fingers. I gasped when I saw him move closer and bend his head down over her pussy. He was going to eat her. I was on fire. I kept up a steady rhythmic pace with my clit.

Looking over to make sure I was watching, Martin stretched out his tongue for a long experimental lick at her begging clitoris. Venus started writhing on the bed when he found it and began tasting her juices. In a few moments, I saw her grab the mattress and dig her fingernails deep into it. She gasped out the sounds of sexual release. "I'm coming," she croaked. I could actually see streams of fluid flow between her legs until the sheet became soaked with her vaginal juices.

Martin's tongue didn't stop even after her cries of passion had subsided. And she didn't asked him to stop, even though she had just climaxed. I had never been able to continue immediately after an orgasm. Seeing her continue to derive pleasure from his tongue sent me over the edge. Before I knew what hit me, I was riding the crest of the wave onto my own orgasm. I kept watching Martin's tongue rolling over her clit. She kept watching me finger-fucking myself as she came again. I could feel Martin's eyes on me, too.

When my orgasm subsided and I returned to earth, Martin was still licking Venus's clit. I couldn't believe the endurance this woman had, to come and come and still allow my lover's tongue to tantalize her. She was moaning and groaning softly while her hips and body responded to each lick on her clit. Martin kept up a steady pace until she began to rise to another climax. I could see Venus's pussy filled with overflowing fluid. Her swollen clit seemed to throb before my eyes.

Finally, he mounted her and slid his cock into her waiting wet pussy, plunging deep and bucking solely for his own pleasure. I could see the thickness of his erection spreading the lips of her sex and driving in to the hilt. His mind seemed to leave the planet, until he was nothing but an erotic body in search of fulfillment. He rocked and rolled on top of her until I could see by the movements of his hips and the contortions of his lips that he was ready to spill another load. I watched fascinated as the man I had come to Vegas with pumped his semen into another woman's body.

After she left, Martin and I lay side by side in the bed, its sheets soaked with a combination of his semen and her vaginal fluids. I rolled in the wetness and felt I was reveling in the sensation of their congress. I described in detail what I had seen, and he described in detail what I had felt. Before long, we were locked together, our bodies connected by his cock driven deep into my pussy.

After that, we knew that we could commit to each other and still have the kind of sex life we would both enjoy. We agreed that we could see and fuck anyone else we wanted, but each of us promised to tell the other everything. A few weeks later, I brought a male friend home and fucked him while Martin watched from a hiding place in the closet. Shortly after that, I brought another man home, and Martin watched openly from a chair at the side of the bed. After that, there was no reason not to get married. So we did.

It's been working out perfectly. We love each other deeply. Each of us finds it exciting to see the other taking pleasure with a casual partner. Neither of us feels any jealousy or resentment. When I fuck another man, Martin feels like he is part of it, whether he's watching or not. I feel the same when he's with another woman.

When either of us watches the other having sex with someone else, both of us can count on a superb erotic experience. We are never disappointed. It is always the highlight of our relationship and always brings out the best in us. All in all, I feel I'm very lucky to have a partner in life who shares the same sexuality as I do. It may be perverted according to ordinary standards, but it's me and it's him, and we're not ashamed.

In a lot of ways, we're better off than most couples. For one thing, we don't have to worry about either of us cheating, because in our kind of relationship, there's no such thing. Not only are we permitted to have sex with others, but each of us is excited about it when the other has an outside lover. We are in absolute agreement that our biggest turn-on is sitting back and watching our mate have sex with another person. I hope your readers will think about the positive aspects of our erotic lifestyle before passing judgment on us.

CONCLUSION

At the beginning of this book, we predicted that you would find, as Shakespeare's Horatio did, that there is more on heaven and earth than was ever dreamt of in your philosophy. We hope that reading this book has helped you make this discovery. As we compiled and edited the stories presented, we learned that our own sexual preferences are not necessarily universal, that what is or is not normal cannot be determined in the confines of our own bedroom.

A John Lennon song recorded by the Beatles declares, "There's nothing you can do that can't be done." What we have learned from writing this book is that there's nothing you can imagine sexually that isn't being done somewhere by someone. Not only that, there's no situation or relationship we can imagine that some group of people has not elevated into a way of life.

We all need food, so we eat certain meals at certain times as part of our everyday lives. Most people need sex, so we make certain acts performed under certain conditions another part of our routine. What the people who told us these stories have in common is that all found ways to make unusual sexual practices the center of their erotic lifestyles. Very little else about them is the same.

Some have made hobbies or occupations of watching others,

while some have built their lives around having others watch them. Some engage in group sex or polyamorous partnerships, while others restrict their sexuality to fantasy and masturbation. There are those who exclude members of their own gender from the pool of potential sex partners, but there are also those who have sex only with members of their own gender, and those who enjoy erotic contact without regard to gender barriers. We see erotic lifestyles lived clandestinely without a spouse's knowledge, but we also see erotic lifestyles based on the inclusion of a domestic partner.

Throughout the book, we encounter entrepreneurs who manage to combine business with pleasure. For some of these, financial compensation is the be-all and end-all, the very thing that makes their erotic contacts exciting. For others, money is much less important than the fact that their business enables them to increase the circle of sex partners and the frequency of sexual experience.

For a different group, the world of business serves only incidentally as the forum in which potential partners may be found. A cook in one of the stories frequently makes dates with customers who come to his restaurant, but his business cannot be characterized as sex-related. The same can be said of a couple who makes a practice of swapping partners with others employed by the same corporation as the husband.

To yet others, business and sex are totally unrelated. They find their partners wherever they happen to be, without relying on their work to provide a source. It is the type of bedmates they seek and the kind of sexuality they enjoy that distinguishes their lifestyles.

We are not recommending that you change the way you live your own erotic life, or even that you experiment with the variations discussed here. If they interest you, the chances are you'll try them without any suggestion from us. If they do not interest you, nothing we said would make a difference. Changing the way you behave was not our purpose.

Our primary object in writing this book was to demonstrate the erotic diversity present in our culture. Since most of us have very little opportunity to know what others regard as exciting or sexually arousing, it was our intention to provide that kind of information. We have tried to serve as a kind of marketplace of erotic practices. Many people who would not be willing to tell their neighbors what they do in bed with their partners are willing to tell us, knowing that we will present the information to the world where it may, after all, be seen by those very same neighbors. Similarly, many people who are curious about how the people on the next street get their pleasures are unwilling and unable to ask. If you have always felt that curiosity, we hope we have helped to satisfy it by sharing stories told to us by those who live on that street.

If you decide to experiment with any of the preferences that others build their lives around, keep in mind your own nature and that of your partner. Some of the people who talked to us said they discovered their unusual tastes late in life. For the most part, however, people choose, early on, the life that suits them best. So if you have not yet tried some of the exotic practices described in this book, it probably means that a lifestyle built around them is not right for you. You may try them and enjoy them occasionally, but in the main you will probably continue living your life the way you have until now.

We think it might be wise at this point for us to say a word or two about safe-sex practices. Outside of your own permanent relationship, engaging in sex without precautions is like playing Russian roulette. The bullet may only be in one chamber of the revolver's cylinder, but if you pull the trigger often enough, it will end up in your brain and kill you. Stopping to describe the way someone puts on a condom or employs some similar form of protection may interrupt the flow of a well-told story, so we usually leave that part out of our narratives. In actual practice, though, there are ways to make taking precautions part of the erotic act and thus an enhancement to pleasure. In any event, we cannot overstress the importance of using whatever is available and appropriate to avoid making the sexual experience a lethal one.

Besides being a demonstration of diversity, we hope that some of the stories in this book will arouse and excite you in a way that contributes to the enjoyment of your own erotic lifestyle. If so, please drop us a line or an e-mail and tell us about it. Who knows? Your sexual experience may one day appear between the covers of one of our books to be enjoyed by readers all over the world between covers of their own.

ATTENTION, READERS

The authors have already begun gathering information for their next book. If you would like to participate by filling out a questionnaire, please get in touch with:

Iris and Steven Finz
P.O. Box 237
The Sea Ranch, CA 95497-0237

Or send an e-mail to:

huck@sexwriters.com

Or visit the authors' website for information and a questionnaire:

www.sexwriters.com